To Kill a Serpent in the Shell

Boris Akunin

TO KILL A SERPENT IN THE SHELL

A Play in Two Acts

Translated from Old Russian,
Buffoonish, and Latin
By Ileana Alexandra Orlich

DALKEY ARCHIVE PRESS

McLean / Dublin

Library of Congress Cataloging-in-Publication Data
Identifiers: ISBN 978-162897-320-4
LC record available at https://lccn.loc.gov/2018058652

Dalkey Archive Press's mission is to publish and preserve literary works from
around the world.

www.dalkeyarchive.com
McLean, IL / Dublin

Printed on permanent/durable acid-free paper.

To Kill a Serpent in the Shell

Introduction

> *And therefore think him as a serpent's egg,*
> *Which, hatch'd, would as his kind grow mischievous,*
> *And kill him in the shell.*
>
> Shakespeare, *Julius Caesar* (Act Two, Scene One)

To Kill a Serpent in the Shell dramatizes the socio-political circumstances immediately prior to the reign of Peter the Great, in the final year of Tsarevna Sofia Alekseyevna's regency (1682-1689), when she ruled Russia with the help of her lover and political ally Vasili Golitsyn. The colloquial, contemporary Russian of the play alternates with passages of the Old Russian of the seventeenth-century tsarist court, the Latin of the enlightened West, and what the author calls "Buffoonish", that is, the carnivalesque discourse of the *skomorox* (itinerant jester, fool, singer, comedian), the voice of the underbelly, of the Russian *narod* (people, folk, nation), whose almost incomprehensible ditty in the opening scene gradually comes into modern linguistic focus to sound like rapping. With a cast of characters whose real-life counterparts are drawn from a historically recognisable fresco of Muscovite society, the play is inextricably bound up with the political and religious milieu of Russia at the time, with the internal politics of Sofia's regency, and, most importantly, with Sofia's image and rule as an inconvenient rival to Peter and his aspirations—a figure often maligned by contemporaries and historians and seldom receiving the credit she deserves.

From the outset, we are introduced to the conflicting political attitudes of the most powerful and influential figures of the period, Princes Vasili Vasilyevich Golitsyn and Boris Alekseyevich Golitsyn, as they sit incognito in a Moscow tavern, gauging the mood of the common people, but each with his own very different conception of the Russian *narod*: Vasili Golitsyn is disdainful of the ruck, but believes in free speech, even when it rises to *lèse-majesté*, whereas Boris Golitsyn believes that free speech, the voice of the people, should be ruthlessly crushed, since "from mockery it's a short road to rebellion". For Vasili Golitsyn, "a man is a man", an individual responsible for his own actions, good or bad, but for Boris Golitsyn, a man is never more than a faceless particle of the nation to which he belongs: a Russian man "is a Russian first and foremost, and only secondarily a man". In Boris Golitsyn's conception, only the nation can be said to be an individual; only the whole has a right to self-determination, for which it must abolish the individuality of its parts. He views the Russian nation as a bear that must be fed, "but not to satiety", given "a little wine now and then, to soothe its soul", and kept on a strong chain. The conflict of ideas in the play arises from the two opposing historical visions embodied by the Golitsyns: Vasili sees Russia as mired in "ignorance, thievery, savagery. A hundred years behind Europe", and wishes to bring about progress through the enactment of rational, enlightened laws, such as the abolition of capital punishment and even sensible traffic regulations; Boris dreams of Russian national greatness and a historical destiny that requires the common people to act as a single non-individualised mass, ruled with an iron fist.

Vasili Golitsyn was the lover and advisor of the regent who styled herself the Great Sovereign Lady Pious Tsarevna and Great Princess Sofia, Autocrat of all the Russias, Great, Little and White. Boris Golitsyn was the tutor of Tsar Peter Alekseyevich, and is said to have played a leading role in the young tsar's eventual bid for power and the overthrow of Tsarevna Sofia. Their tavern conversation in Akunin's play, which offers a close-up view of the Russian people – pious, Orthodox folk, "good-humoured, even when drunk", but dangerous when angry – is interrupted by the arrival of the fool, leading a bear on a chain, and a flute player. Together, they address the "Christian brothers" and promise a mock-overview of "how Mother Russia's getting along". Chief among the "crazy things going down round here", they claim, is having two tsars on the throne of Russia, a diarchy resulting from unforeseen circumstances and as politically preposterous, in their words, as having, "two suns shining or two moons silvering together in the sky".

The death without male issue of sickly Tsar Fyodor

in 1682 at the age of twenty had left his brother Ivan V, the son of Tsar Aleksey from his first marriage to Maria Miloslavskaya, and his half-brother, Peter, son of Tsar Aleksey from his second marriage to Natalya Naryshkina, as legitimate heirs. Patriarch Joachim's swift decision to assemble bishops, boyars, lords-in-waiting, and a host of councillors and people from all the ranks of the Kremlin in order to ask which of the two *tsareviches* should rule generated a violent, though not entirely unpredictable, conflict. Given Ivan's "feeble-mindedness and other mental and corporeal handicaps", the crowd appeared to favour the younger, underage brother Peter. This choice triggered an angry response on the part of Moscow's armed guard, known as the *streltsy*[1], who, incited by the rumour that the older brother Ivan had been murdered by the Naryshkins, stormed the Kremlin palace and murdered two of the brothers of Peter's mother Natalya Naryshkina.

As the sister of Ivan, the older *tsarevich* who was perceived by the angry *streltsy* to be the rightful heir to the throne, the young Tsarevna Sofia had every right to support and defend him. Moreover, many believed that she also played an important role in protecting Peter and his mother, who barely escaped death at the hands of the *streltsy*. There were also accusers, such as historian Andrei Artamonovich Matveyev (1666-1728), whose

---

[1] The *streltsy*, or musketeers, had been founded in the reign of Ivan IV (the Terrible), in the middle of the sixteenth century. In 1682, when their number had reached about 55,000 men, they played a vital role in bringing Sofia to power.

father had been killed in the 1682 attack by the *streltsy*. In Matveyev's view, although Sofia may have looked like she was protecting the Naryshkins from the *streltsy*, she was in fact the protagonist of "the most profound Italian politics, where they say one thing and mean another".[2]

As it turned out, the rebellion of the *streltsy* was indeed a battle cry for Tsarevna Sofia's own campaign to become a regent in the dual tsardom, which seemed a sensible political compromise to appease the *streltsy*. The joint names of the two half-brothers acting as sovereign tsars and great princes were formally acknowledged and honoured in the form of the double throne that can still be seen in the Armoury Museum of the Kremlin. Through the curtained window in the back of the throne, regent Sofia is said to have whispered instructions to the two tsars, one feeble-minded, the other a minor.

Art of the period illustrated the political triad of the two brothers ruling jointly under Sofia's governance, such as the 1683 allegorical portrait of Tsars Ivan and Peter by the Ukrainian Ivan Shchirsky, which depicts the brothers being blessed by Christ and, above them, a maiden with eagle wings being crowned from heaven – a symbol of the Holy Wisdom (Sophia) protecting and guarding the young tsars in their handling of the country's tangled affairs. Rumoured to have run affairs of the state even earlier on, at her brother Tsar Fyodor's

---

[2]A. A. Matveev, '*Zapiski Andreia Artamonovicha grafa Matveeva*,' in N. Sakharov, ed. *Zapiski russkix ljudej Sobotyia vremen Petra Velikogo*, St. Petersburg, 1841, 30.

bedside, Sofia was now a ruler in her own right, as indicated in her official title of Autocrat, which she had added to her name by 1686.

As the French historian and novelist Henry Troyat points out in a recent re-examination of the situation:

> the formidable Sofia was . . . to be reckoned with. Having tasted the life of a free woman at her brother Fyodor's side, caring for him and advising him, she refused to contemplate a return to the *terem*, that gynaeceum of another age . . . Sofia wanted to live, to love, to dominate.[3]

During the Petrine cult, when Peter the Great was typically seen as akin to God, historians habitually denied Sofia's merits and found her to be a mere shadow of Peter's greatness, consumed with a self-destructive love of power. In the *Pantheon of Russian Authors* first published in 1802, N.M. Kuramzin writes:

> Sofia was one of the greatest women Russia ever produced. Suffice it to say that in respect of her mind and intellectual qualities she was worthy of the name of sister of Peter the Great; but blinded by ambition, she aspired to rule alone and to reign alone, thus placing the historian under the sad obligation of being her accuser.[4]

---

[3]H. Troyat, *Peter the Great*, London, 1987. 13. Translated from *Peter Le Grand*, 1979.

[4]N. M. Karamzin, *Panteon rossijskix avtorov*, in *Sochineniia v dvux tomax*, vol. 2 Leningrad, 1984, 102. He also writes about Sofia as author and playwright, pp.172-3.

In the light of such partial rehabilitation of Sofia, Akunin's play foregrounds an interesting dramatic conflict that relies on historical testimony to take a closer look at the tsarevna and the regency as a hiatus in the long history of Russia's autocratic rule. In *Histoire de Russie* (1782), for example, the French historian M. Levesque denies Sofia's involvement in the rebellion of 1682 ("It has not been proven that she was responsible for the *streltsy* revolt which does not even appear to have been premeditated"); the rebellion of 1689 ("She felt the same horror over the *streltsy* plot as the rest of the nation."); and the rebellion of 1698 ("She had been overthrown; Peter reigned alone, but she was missed. He would have had to blot out Sofia's memory in order to make himself agreeable to the nation").[5] Significantly, Levesque further writes:

> It was a great boon for the country that she took the helm of the state, which could otherwise only have been governed either by a prince whose feebleness bordered on the imbecilic, or a child who had no one but a young inexperienced mother to support him on the throne".[6]

As the events leading to her overthrow take center stage, the play sets out to regard Sofia favourably for ultimately rejecting the opportunity to eliminate Peter, even though she knew that she would be sacrificed in the ensuing power struggle and that her legacy, whose

[5]M. Levesque, *Histoire de Russie*, vol. 4, Paris 1782. Pp 78, 102, 152.
[6]Ibid. 103.

values were inverted in the historical writings of autocratic rule, would be blotted out and mystified while
Peter would lay claim to an imperial Russian history
going back to Ivan the Terrible.

Tsarevna Sofia Alekseyevna

Born in Moscow in 1657, the infant Sofia was recorded
in official documents as the Sovereign Lady Tsarevna
and Great Princess Sofia Alekseyevna. She was the sixth
child and fourth daughter of the Sovereign Tsar and
Great Prince Aleksey Mikhailovich, Autocrat of all the
Russias, Great, Little and White, and his wife Maria
Ilyinichna Miloslavskaya.

The second ruler of the Romanov line, Tsar Aleksey
Mikhailovich (1645-1676) was the son of Tsar Mikhail
Fyodorovich (1613-1645), a man of modest social
standing who had been elected to the throne of Russia,
or Muscovy, as foreigners most commonly called the
country, following the Times of Troubles (1589-1612)
when succession had been under dispute.

By the time Sofia was born, Tsar Aleksey had survived a popular revolt against corrupt officials and unfair
taxes, had led a successful campaign in Lithuania and
Livonia, and had issued a new legal code. A protector of Orthodox Christianity and gifted "manager of
men",[7] Tsar Aleksey nurtured an emancipatory vision
for Russia. According to his English physician Samuel
Collins, the tsar's campaign in Poland and his visits to

---

[7]Philips Longworth, *Alexis, Tsar of all the Russias*, London, 1984, 244.

towns whose Gothic, Renaissance, and Baroque architecture was significantly more sophisticated than that of Russia's towns, led him "to model his court and edifices more stately, to furnish his rooms with tapestry and to contrive houses of pleasure abroad".[8] In 1675 the tsar ordered the Englishman John Hebdon, one of his agents abroad, to bring back "tapestries and furniture, musical boxes, laces and tableware, singing birds and carriages".[9] A year after his marriage to Natalya Naryshkina, in 1672 Tsar Aleksey ordered preparations for the first court theatrical performance in Russia's history, held in the Preobrazhenskoe Palace. Performed in German by the boys of the Foreign Quarter of the Lutheran parish, the tragi-comedy of *Ahasuerus and Esther* appeared to the transfixed tsar and his court as extraordinarily artistic, with music, costumes, and the fascination of the stage which the very young Tsarevna Sofia, along with the other children and the new Tsaritsa Natalia, watched "through a grille, or rather through chinks in specially boarded-off premises", according to Dr. Laurent Rinhuber of Saxony, who was also in attendance.[10]

The tsar's ambitions and the vision-broadening experiences he offered to his court – with nine different theatrical performances, one ballet accompanied by organs, viols, and dances presented over the course of three and a half years – are indicative of his ambivalence when

---

[8]S. Collins, *The Present State of Russia*, London, 1671, 64-5.

[9]Longworth, Alexis, *Tsar of all the Russias*, London, 1984, 134.

[10]Reutenfels, *Skazanie*, 1905, book 3, 83.

it came to choosing between Byzantine traditionalism and the attractions of the Western world. They were also characteristic of the environment in which Sofia was raised, and remained unresolved conflicts of her regency (1682-1689).

Like the other women in the tsar's immediate family and circle whose lives were narrowly confined within the cloistered *terem*,[11] Sofia spent her childhood and early youth away from the public eye until the death of Tsar Aleksey. She began to gain notoriety during the short reign of her brother, Fyodor, after whose death she emerged as the regent and *de facto* ruler of Russia in 1682. Overthrown in 1689 by her younger half-brother, who was later to become Peter the Great, Sofia was sent to the Novodevichy Convent, where she lived in a confinement that reached its critical point when the belief that she had played a part in the failed attempt to depose Tsar Peter during the *streltsy* rebellion of 1698 forced her to retire into complete seclusion, taking monastic vows under the name Susanna. She died and was buried at the Novodevichy Convent in the Church of the Immaculate Lady of Smolensk in 1704.

Appointed regent of Russia in an unprecedented way,

---

[11]The apartments in which the women of the tsar's family spent their lives in almost complete seclusion. Of a strictness and restraint that probably exceeded the regulations of a convent, the *terem* emphasised a monastic way of life composed of endless prayer and work on embroideries of vestments and altar clothes bequeathed to the palace churches and convents that enjoyed royal patronage.

the young Sofia was already an educated woman, having been tutored, like her brothers Fyodor and Ivan, by the late Simeon Polotsky, known for his Latinising tendencies. After Polotsky's death in 1680, Sofia had turned to his successor, Sylvester Medvedev, a prelate who based his theological studies on Polish Catholic sources and was far better educated and more sophisticated than Patriarch Joachim. Having founded the Moscow Academy, Sofia promoted the cultivation of *belles lettres* and even had a reputation as a playwright. She was also politically ambitious and, relatively quickly, became the real source of authority in the palace. Commenting on the members of the Kremlin royal family in the year of 1683, an anonymous Polish diarist remarked that

> She rules in Moscow with the boyars having raised her brother Ivan to the throne . . . She guards Ivan so well that he never goes anywhere and no one visits him without her leave. The boyar councils likewise could not be called without her, both on affairs of state and for private cases.[12]

In the opinion of the Austrian envoy Johann Eberhardt Hövel who visited the tsar's court in 1684, Sofia was perceived to have "a firm grip on the government . . . and [was] said to possess great wit and judgement". She also seemed to have increasingly appropriated the tsars' roles since, in Hövel's view, the older brother Ivan was "a puppet ruler" and Peter, who had

---

[12] *Diariusz zaboystwa tyranskjego senatorow moskiewskich w stolicy ruku 1682 y o obraniu dwoch carow Ioanna y Piotra*, St. Petersburg, 1901, 13.

"the greater support from the boyars and magnates",[13] was still a minor.

By the time of the Treaty of Eternal Peace with Poland in 1686, Sofia had been recognized as the only source of authority in the Kremlin, with Golitsyn as an equal match to her governing ability and with Shaklovity, director of the feared *streltsy*, eager to serve and please her. In *To Kill a Serpent in the Egg*, Boris Golitsyn, a relative of Vasili and sworn enemy of the tsarevna, who, as in real life, plots her overthrow so that Peter can seize the throne, calls the two "the mind" (Vasili Golitsyn) and "the fist" (Shaklovity), or "the dreamer" and "the cast-iron noggin", respectively.

Aside from the Kremlin inner circle, foreigners were fully aware of the tsarevna's power and often praised it. Georg Adam Schlessing, who published an early version of his views in 1687, stated that although Ivan and Peter occupied the throne, neither of them made any decisions, and everything was decided by Sofia: "It is as clear as day to many people", writes Schlessing, "that she is gifted with a high degree of governing".[14]

Sofia's self-aggrandisement in politics is documented by various portraits that inaugurate, according to

---

[13]Quoted in F. Andelung, *Kritischliterärische Übersicht der Reisenden in Russland bis* 1700, vol. 2, St. Petersburg and Leipzig, 1846, pp.370-1.

[14]"*Die Gantze Beschreibung Reusslandts*" (1687), trans. L. Lapteva as "*Rasskaz očevidca o žizni Moskovij konca XVII, veka*", Voprosy istorij, 1970, no.1, 111.

Lindsey Hughes, the realistic portrayal of women in the history of Russian culture.[15] The political status of Sofia is echoed in the so-called eagle portrait of 1689, based on a print by the Ukrainian engraver Leon Tarasevich, in which her portrait appears within an oval frame set on the breast of a double-headed eagle; the rim of the oval bears the legend "The most illustrious and sovereign, by the Grace of God, Great Sovereign Lady, Pious Tsarevna and Great Princess Sofia Alekseyevna, Autocrat of the Great, Little and White Russians". Depicted in the laudatory pose reserved for tsars and serving as testimonial to her being a ruler in her own right – with a legitimate claim to royal titles and equal in status to her brothers – this portrait shows Sofia holding a sceptre in her right hand and an orb in her left, with part of the Kremlin appearing behind her. As Hughes points out, the use of the oval frame as well as the pose with the orb and sceptre are derived from the *Book of Crowned Head* or *Titles* (*Titulyarnik*), compiled in the tsar's Foreign Office in 1672, which in turn provided the model for the 1682 coronation images of Ivan and Peter. The political message of the portrait reaches full significance in the case of the Bloteling engravings, which are a series of prints made after Tarasevich's oval portrait (minus the eagle surroundings) which was taken to Holland in 1689 by the Foreign Office Secretary Andrei Vinius and

---

[15]For this and for a wealth of information on Tsarevna Sofia's regency, see Lindsey Hugues's seminal book, *Sofia: Regent of Russia 1657 – 1704*, Yale UP, 1990. 141-2.

eventually became the version reworked by the artist
Abraham Bloteling "in order that the great sovereign
lady should enjoy fame overseas".[16] Most likely, the one
hundred prints sent back to Russia reached the country
after the tsarevna's overthrow and, as Hugues estimates,
were destroyed by order of Peter, with only copies outside Russia surviving.

Prince Vasili Vasilyevich Golitsyn

By all accounts, Prince Vasili Vasilyevich Golitsyn was
the most prominent member of Sofia's entourage. The
influential French commentator Foy de la Neuville, who
appears as a character in *To Kill a Serpent in the Shell*,
and whose account of his visit to Moscow in 1689 as
the agent of the King of Poland was published in 1898,
pronounced Golitsyn to be "without contradiction one
of the most spirited, most refined, and most liberal men
this country has ever seen".[17] As noted by historians, La
Neuville's praise of Golitsyn is grossly exaggerated, as
demonstrated by his description of Golitsyn's mansion
as "one of the most magnificent in Europe",[18] when in
reality it was fairly average by Western standards. This is
certainly magnified for stage effect in Akunin's play, in
which Golitsyn and La Neuville speak to each other in

---

[16]A. P. Bogdanov, *Političeskaja gravjura i Rossij perioda regenctva Sofia
Alekseevny, Istočnikovedenie otečestvennoj istorij*, Moscow, 1981. 245.

[17]*Dopolnenija k aktam istoričeskim*, vol. 10, no. 74, 312-13.

[18]Neuville, F. de la, *Relation curieuse et nouvelle de Moscovie*, The
Hague, 1699, 177.

Latin and the Russian boyar makes humorously clear his ambivalent status as to Russia's domestic policy.

A member of one of Moscow's distinguished families and a boyar since 1676, Prince Vasili Golitsyn rose to prominence during Tsar Fyodor's reign, when Sofia most likely valued his support for her brother Tsar Fyodor's policies and relied on his counsel. Among other political initiatives that must have caught Sofia's attention was Golitsyn's willingness to discard the court practice of making appointments on the basis of a candidate's lineage and the service records of his ancestors, a change that drew the anger of the upper nobility to which he himself belonged. His documented association with Sofia began in May 1682 when he was appointed Director of the Foreign Office. In that role, he relied on his contacts and his postings during Tsar Fyodor's reign, which had familiarised him with operations in the Ukraine against the Turks and Tatars (1676-8), operations which were at the core of foreign policy during the regency.

Like Sofia, Golitsyn had a prominent political profile that extended abroad, and was close to foreigners from whom he obtained memoranda on how to proceed on various issues, such as his commitment to reform the Russian army through measures that formed the basis of Peter's reforms.

Closely related to Sofia's oval portraits and most likely also the work of Tarasevich is the engraving of Vasili Golitsyn commissioned in 1687, just before the first Crimean campaign and postdating the 1686 Treaty of Eternal Peace with Poland, which was one of Golitsyn's greatest achievements. Accompanied by a coat of arms and lines of poetry that may have been composed by Sofia, the portrait depicts Golitsyn holding a hetman's mace after the fashion of Polish portraits of the period and may be regarded politically as a male counterpart of Sofia's portrait, both conforming to the subtle trapping of rulership during the Regency.

Fyodor Leontevich Shaklovity

Another important member of Sofia's inner circle during the regency who plays an important part in Akunin's play is Fyodor Leontevich Shaklovity. Having started his career in Tsar Aleksey's Secret Chancellery, by 1682 Shaklovity had become Director of the important Streltsy Department, even though he was not an aristocrat. He became close to Sofia during that year's three-day rebellion of the *streltsy*, when preference for the young Peter on the part of the crowd and certain boyars was interpreted by the *streltsy* as bypassing Ivan's rights. To be sure, the *streltsy* outburst of naïve attachment to legitimacy was in no way revolutionary; quite the opposite, it sought to validate their political alliances with the monarchic order, since the *streltsy* selfishly feared the Naryshkins as the new masters. According to the memoir of Heinrich Butenant, a German commercial agent of the King of Denmark and a witness to the 1682 rebellion,

Throughout the three days that this rebellion lasted they did everything in the name of Tsar Ivan Alekseyevich, although of course the *streltsy* did not ask anyone, and they did everything according to their own will.[19]

The disagreements between the two young tsareviches' factions and the *streltsy* rebellion, which led to the dual monarchy and allowed Sofia to wield political power, also sealed and secured Shaklovity's increasingly important role, matched by the intensity and dramatic colouring of his devotion during the regency. Famously, in 1687, when Ukrainian colonels delivered an oration to the underage tsars, Shaklovity commissioned a panegyric for Sofia too, which was accompanied by an engraved portrait, so that she would not feel slighted but receive equal praise.[20]

The Power Struggle

By 1688, however, several years into the regency, the sixteen-year-old Peter began to be officially groomed for power. He started to attend council meetings and was rumoured to have even visited the chancelleries at night. He embarked upon promoting his Naryshkin relatives to the Duma and, after marrying Yevdokia Lopukhina in 1689, began promoting her family, too, while Sofia

---

[19]Butenant, "Mutiny in Moscow, 1682: A Contemporary Account", trans. J. Keep, Canadian Slavonic Papers, 23, 1981, 410-42.

[20]Bogdanov, "*Političeskaia gravjura v Rossij perioda regenctva Sofi Alekseevny*". *Istočnikovedenie otečestvennoj istorij*. Moscow, 1982. 238-9.

was powerless to block their political advancement and influence.

With the imminent second Crimean campaign in the autumn of 1688 and the court preparations for it that highlighted Sofia's leadership and Golitsyn's service, Tsar Peter took part in a separate, elaborate religious ceremony with the Patriarch, aimed at sidelining the tsarevna and placing the young tsar in a favourable light. He was the tall, handsome tsar, clearly a better choice than his feeble brother guarded by his female protector, Tsarevna Sofia. Projecting himself to the public as the protector of Orthodoxy, the young tsar processed through the Kremlin cathedrals, visited Red Square, and entered the Cathedral of Our Lady of Kazan before returning to the Kremlin.

Within a few months, in early 1689, the younger tsar married Yevdokiya Lopukhina, and engaged in extensive diplomatic activities, such as receiving the ambassadors from Brandenburg and Jesuits from France. One such visitor was the Jesuit Père Phillip Avril, who arrived in Moscow in 1689 bearing a letter from Louis XIV asking for free passage to China. Although this request was denied, Father Avril spent some time at the court, indicating in his *Travels into divers Parts of Europe and Asia*, published in London in 1693, that Vasili Golitsyn no longer played an important part in the affairs of the court, had too many enemies, and had survived two assassination attempts. Incorporated in the play, such an attempt on Vasili Golitsyn's life echoes just as realistically the atmosphere of the run-up to the tsarevna's overthrow, foreshadowed in Boris Golitsyn's admonition to Vasili/Vasya to give up the power:

> While you and Sofia have been canoodling and composing sagacious treatises, Peter has grown up. He is now a married man. By law and by custom he should be ruling already, but instead our ruler is a girl. How long will this go on? Think about it, Vasya. The two of you are going to have to give up power, and then where are you going to hide? Better you do so willingly.

In the meantime, away from the intrigues and power games going on in the Kremlin, the Moscow crowds, as the play's opening suggests, were highly entertained by the way things looked, especially in the case of the "two Tsars Alekseyevitch, / The one weirder than the other". Alluding to Ivan's numerous handicaps and overall feeble-mindedness, the fool's chant scorns the older tsar for being "God's little birdie, a childlike soul. He's able to sit in the golden room. But as he's sick, he plays with the dolls there". Faring no better, as rumours were rife regarding his play-military and naval exploits, younger Peter Alekseyevitch is mocked for his training and drilling of the so-called play regiments – the Preobrazhensky and Semenovsky Guards – for his having "a bent for German sort of stuff", and his interest in shipbuilding.

The crowd's view of Vasili Golitsyn is even more amusing. Publicly scorned after the two failed campaigns to Crimea, he is derided in the fool's song:

Off to war the heroic Vaska goes
He wants to conquer the Crimea.
But when he got there, they kicked his arse,
And he ran blubbing all the way home.

Vulgar and denigrating, the tavern rabble's perception of Sofia, who is the next object of general mockery, stems from her love affair with Golitsyn, a doubly bold and unpardonable offense since he was married with three children. Her reputedly unattractive appearance, a public perception made widespread thanks to Foy de la Neuville's description of her, is most likely the source for public ridicule. Even though it is unlikely that the Frenchman ever saw Sofia in person, he portrays her as being "of a monstrous size, with a head as big as a bushel, with hair on her face, growths on her legs, and at least forty years old".[21] Since Sofia was only thirty-two in 1689, when Neuville wrote his impression of her, there are reasons to question his account; nevertheless, Neuville's description stands for public consumption as the overwhelmingly accepted appearance of Sofia. In the play, the fool puts a woman's headdress on the bear, which begins to mimic Sofia, and then refers to her as:

an old hag [who] now rules the Rooshian state,
Bitch Sonya, the Muscovite princess . . .
Burly, shameless old hag that she is,
She canoodles with Vasya Golitsyn
The saviour of this nation of ours.

---

[21]Neuville, F. de la, "*Relations curieuse et nouvelle de Moscovie*", *Recit de mon voyage*, 151.

On this noisy and gossipy note, the brawling space of the late seventeenth-century Moscow tavern echoes the liberties made possible by young Peter's "Drunken Synod of Fools and Jesters", in which the tsar and his retinue indulged in obscene ceremonies, poking fun at various aspects of the Muscovite scene. The tavern debauchery also reveals in visible and audible terms the particular atmosphere of that socio-political regime, with its specific cultural patterns, court intrigues, and bawdy brawls. In the next dramatic intervention, the conversation between the two Golitsyns moves beyond the tavern teeming with the raucous crowd; their dialogue, articulated in terms of interactions and reactions between their respective views, offers an intriguing historical perspective not only on the immediate political scene, but also on the Russian people and the country's aegis of autocracy.

From the start, the two interlocutors delineate their diverging stand on government issues. When Vasili Golitsyn asks the menacing *streltsy*, who have arrested the tavern entertainers, the fool and the flute player, to let them go, Boris Golitsyn states angrily that those who "made a mockery of the authorities [and] insulted the rulers" should have their tongues cut out. Having used his influence to ensure that the two are released, Vasili Golitsyn also expresses his further regret at having failed to repeal such practices of mutilation because the boyars had ruled against it. True to his political convictions that he is presumably imparting to his ward, the young Tsar

Peter, Boris replies: "the boyars were right to vote against it. The common folk should treat the authorities with respect as their own mothers. From mockery it's a short road to rebellion".

The incident and Vasili Golitsyn's intervention lend credence to contemporary reports, such as that of Father Philippe Avril, who writes that Golitsyn "was undoubtedly the most accomplished, and most knowing Lord at the Court of Moscow, he loved Strangers, and particularly the French, because the Noble sentiments he had observed in them, were very consonant to his own".[22] Juxtaposed with Vasili's embrace of Western values (the boyar and his son were rumoured to wear miniatures of Louis XIV on their sashes), Boris Golitsyn's crude remarks provide both a justification for the iron-fisted laws and inhuman practices of the tsars from the days of Tsar Ivan IV (1533-1584, better known as *Grozny*, the Terrible) and a foreshadowing of things to come. Associated with territorial conquest, imperial domination, and harsh punishments of political unrest, foes and court intrigues, Ivan IV was widely perceived as the prototypical mediaeval, autocratic tsar, consistently portrayed by Russians as a providential leader despite his cruelty. His murderous exploits and civil abuses are seen

[22]Avril, P., *Travels into divers Parts of Europe and Asia* (Undertaken by the French King's Order to discover a new way by Land into China), Book 4, London, 1693. 55-6. Trans. from *Voyages en divers états d'Europe and d'Asie entrepris pour découvrir un nouveau chemin à la Chine*, Paris, 1692.

in historical context as an apologia for the greatness of Russia, the country and its people, even as a controlling discipline necessary to secure the pursuit of Christian values and Orthodox tradition that had been extended beyond Byzantium to a Moscow that was to achieve glory as the third Rome.[23]

When the captain of the *streltsy*, upon recognizing him, addresses Vasili Golitsyn as "the helmsman of the affairs of the state" and states that he will take his orders from this Golitsyn only, the sarcastic ire of Boris Golitsyn who mutters that "Tsar Peter's boyards are not held in esteem", brings the play to a climactic point of historical significance. The country is now run by two warring factions: on the one hand, Regent Sofia guided by Vasily Golitsyn; on the other, the faction supporting

[23]After the final victory against the khanates of Kazan and Astrakhan in the 1550s, Ivan the Terrible ordered the construction of a new cathedral on the Red Square. Originally named the Intercession of the Virgin or the Cathedral of Our Lady of Kazan, in honor of the sacred feast day when Ivan IV had captured the Tatar capital of Kazan, St. Basil's Church marked the triumph of the Orthodox traditions of Byzantium and signalled Moscow's rise as the new Rome that was to lead the religious war against the Mongol-Tatar raids from the steppes. To many of the Russian faithful, Moscow was a successor to Rome and Constantinople, with the gold-domed St. Basil's Church an immediate counterpart and heir to Hagia Sofia after Constantinople had fallen to the Turks in 1453. In time, Moscow's embrace of Orthodoxy was cemented by the city's 200 documented churches and monasteries until the fires of 1821 during Napoleon's occupation.

Tsar Peter, who is about to come of age and is being groomed to take over the throne. The time of the play, presumably the year 1689, acquires increased dramatic intensity through the ensuing conversation between the two Golitsyns. As they are leaving the tavern, their dialogue highlights the political and historical context that foreshadows the end of Sofia's regency.

With all its promises of liberal policies and reorientation toward the Western values that Golitsyn favoured, the regency is in its final showdown with the challenges of a different type of governance, as suggested in Boris Golitsyn's views, which are to be passed on to his ward, Tsar Peter, and to Russia's subsequent rulers.

For example, to Vasili's question "What is the most important thing in a Russian Man?", Boris's reply that "He is a Russian first and foremost, and only secondarily a man" foreshadows, as we have seen above, a form of social organisation based on the suppression and ultimate elimination of the individual. Further, as Boris explains, the Russian people:

> are like the fool's pet bear. Underfeed it and it will grow surly. Overfeed it and it will grow stubborn and cease to dance to your flute. There are four rules. The bear will follow whomever adheres to them. The first rule: feed it, but not to satiety. The second: play an intricate tune on your flute, so it will want to dance. The third: let it drink a little now and then, to soothe its soul. And the final rule, the most interesting of all . . . keep it on a strong chain.

Aware of the vicious political intrigues, Vasili remarks that the Naryshkins are dreaming of deposing the regent Sofia and seizing control of a backward and benighted state. Boris's reply is chilling:

Let me tell you what we'll do when my ward Petrusha becomes a true autocrat. Russians are not Romans; they don't require much bread or many circuses. But they do need a great aim, and we shall give them one. Rather than a flute to whose merry tune they might dance. A great aim is a chain. A stout one. One nation is great, it can move mountains if it is guided wisely. You call us backward? No problem, we'll catch up. From Europe we'll adopt what is beneficial and reject what is harmful.

Genuinely puzzled about what could be harmful in Europe, Vasili does not have to wait too long for an answer. Boris's reply comes with total self-assurance:

Because over there everything is all over the place. Everybody thinks whatever he likes. He goes wherever he wants. But over here there will be a single will: the state's. And a single mind . . . Of greatness. Taken in himself, a man is petty, self-seeking, he snuffles around the ground looking for food, like a mouse. But when men come together, united as a nation, they become great. This is why rule is required; this is why the state is required.

Vasili's remark that "a country's greatness resides in the happiness of its inhabitants", meets with Boris's scorn. Urging Vasili "to wake up", Boris points out that,

This is Russia, not Holland. That sort of thing never existed here, and it never will. You are clever, cleverer than any of us, but you've got your head in the clouds. Let's build what we can build down here, on the ground, not castles in the sky . . . Verily it is written: No ruler more dangerous than the dreamer. But why do you think that people should live happily? In which of the Gospels is it written? Man must fulfil his purpose and endure suffering without complaint. Ask the Patriarch or whomever you wish. Here in Russia greatness lies not in happiness, but happiness in greatness. If everybody started caring about his own personal happiness, what would become of Russia?

The dialogue between the two cousins throws into sharp relief the two radically different options facing Russia, as embodied in the Sofia/Peter dichotomy. The dramatic differences between their approaches to ruling Russia mark a departure from such views as that of nineteenth-century historian D. Mordovtsev, who claimed that the regency and Peter's reign were both part of the same smooth, natural flow of Russian history.[24] In Mordovtsev's view "Sofia was the first to leave the *terem* and to open the doors of that *terem* for all Russian women who so desired it, just as her younger brother Peter later opened a window onto Europe".

As Akunin's play suggests, the legacy of Russia would

---

[24]Mordovtsev, D., *Russkie istoričeskie ženščiny. Populjarnye rasskazy iz russkoj žizni*, St. Petersburg, 1874, 306-7.

have been quite different if Sofia's embrace of liberating practices, no matter how light, coupled with Vasili Golitsyn's growing receptiveness to Western values, had prevailed. *To Kill a Serpent in the Shell* stages the strong, diametrically-opposed contradictions between the two Golitsyns that seem to embody the antipodes of, on the one hand, Westernising Russia by taking small steps in the direction that Tsarevna Sofia's regency proposes, and, on the other, keeping the country aligned with the practices of mediaeval Russia through the autocracy of Tsar Peter's rule – the course that eventually prevailed. With the benefit of historical hindsight, the continuity of Peter's totalitarian practices can be seen – in the linear temporality of historical causality – in twentieth-century Soviet, and contemporary, Russia.

Absolutism was the *sine qua non* condition of the rule of Peter and later Stalin – an absolutism so entrenched that it never gave way to any form of political plurality, as happened elsewhere in Western Europe. As autocratic leaders of the most absolutist state in Europe, in spite of their ambitions to bring Russia in line with the rest of Europe, Tsar Peter, the Romanovs, and later Stalin ruled over an overwhelmingly agrarian and underpopulated country, with no great cities in the European sense, historically and culturally isolated from the world and impossible to Westernise as long as its people lived the Russian way of life. Although by the late sixteenth century Russia was no longer isolated, Europeans tended to regard it as a religious civilisation, with monastic

learning and icons everywhere, rooted in spiritual traditions of the Eastern Orthodox Church, going back to
Byzantium and the prophecy of Moscow as the third
Rome. Tsar Peter's rule, and the Soviet Union much
later, did not bring much to the dark and backward
customs of Russia's past, and the people remained much
the same. Tsar Peter's project of cultural engineering to
reconstruct the Russians as Europeans had as much suc-
cess as Stalin's attempt to engineer the soul of the Soviet
people to make it the vanguard of socialism.

To a certain extent, then, Akunin's play is an inter-
rogation of history that looks at the rulers themselves
both as individuals and collectively, within their immediate circle and background, in order to examine the
scale of values by which each would have ruled and the
historical context each of them embraced in the process
of determining Russia's future socio-political course. In
the immediate space of the play, which predates Sofia's
overthrow in 1689, the humanist values of Prince Vasili
Golitsyn seem politically inadequate. Change appears
to be on its way in the form of the young Peter, still a
serpent inside the shell and mentored by the likes of
Boris Golitsyn, who marches impatiently to the drum
of Russia's greatness to fulfil his own ambitions.

By inviting a nostalgic glance at the twilight of
Tsarevna Sofia's regency, however, Akunin's play cap-
tures more than a time shaped by political rivalries
and warring factions. While steering from the known
course of history, *To Kill a Serpent in the Shell* offers

a socio-historical and psychological study that trans-
fers the characters and social milieu from one set of
historical circumstances to another by relying on the
stage-protected circulation of fantasy. In the imagined
world of the stage, the play features a fateful encounter
between two socially and politically opposing ideologies,
superimposed in a double scenario filtered through a
third, voyeuristic eye, a dramatic process suggested in
the fictional character of Tryokhglazov, whose name in
Russian means "Three-Eyes". One scenario shows an
anxious Sofia, the tsarevna eager to bring to fruition the
transformations of an incipient humanism promoted by
Golitsyn and to secure Shaklovity's help to kill young
Peter, the serpent in the shell, before the egg is hatched
and the venom is spewed out. The other scenario features an exuberant Boris Golitsyn hailing the greatness of his ward, the young Tsar Peter, whose foretold
embrace of totalitarian rule after removing Sofia and
Vasili Golitsyn and executing the *streltsy*, marks a violent
and irreversible return to Russia's tradition of autocracy
and of achieving a greatness predicated on cruelty and
human sacrifice, such as in forced-labour sites like the
marshes on which Tsar Peter built St. Petersburg or the
deserted steppe where Stalin built Magnitogorsk.

The first of the play's imagined scenarios finds its
justification in contemporary documents that give
high praise to Sofia's regency and Vasili Golitsyn's role
as Minister of State. According to Prince Boris Kurakin,
during that time the government "was administered

with great energy and justice, and was much to the people's liking; never had there been such a wise regime in the Russian realm. And during the seven years of her rule the country reached a pinnacle of prosperity".[25] Also based on the testimony of the period, the play projects Vasili Golitsyn's character as forward-thinking and reform-oriented. In an imaginary on-stage interview, he meets the historically acknowledged La Neuville to express his views of the things that need to be done to achieve a thriving Russian state:

> Above all else, the peasants need to be emancipated from serfdom, because good citizens cannot come from slaves. Let every man plough his own land, but also pay the treasury a tax according to his means . . . We will invite the children of the nobility to attend schools. A modern state is impossible without an educated class. The eighteenth century is just around the corner, after all. We will establish embassies in every foreign capital. When neighbours get along with each other, there are fewer wars and trade is more profitable. We will rebuild our wooden cities in stone, to prevent them from burning to the ground whenever there is a hot summer. We will forbid the persecution of those of other faiths. There are many ethnic groups in our state; let nobody feel a foreigner in Russia.

[25]Prince B. I. Kurakin, "*Gistorija o care Petre Akeekseviče 1682-1694*" in *Rossju podnjal na dyby. Istoria otečestva v romanax, povestiax, documentax. Veka XVII-XVIII*, vol. 1, Moscow 1987, 364-5.

Even in this dramatic, highly hypothetical mode, comically juxtaposed with an aberrant scenario in which the Prince makes fun of the cruel practices of the period, Golitsyn's character confesses that the way he thinks is, unfortunately, only the way the people and the country ought to be, and that he is "imagining something that doesn't exist". In this imagined scenario of the play, Tryokhglazov shoots young Peter and calmly states that "The serpent will bite no more" while Boris Golitsyn laments the slaying and what he perceives to be the lost "greatness for Russia":

Now there will be nothing. Nothing to dream of. No fleet. No victories. No windows on Europe. No regulation capital on the seashore. No empire . . .

For a brief moment marked in the imagined world of the stage by a sense of the performance being over and of the spotlight fading on the dead Peter, it seems possible that Russia might actually have been a different country, governed judiciously and wisely by the political alliance of Golitsyn and Tsarevna Sofia.

Was theirs a political association and virtuous attachment only? The extent of their personal relationship is difficult to fathom, although some terms of endearment from the coded letters the tsarevna sent to Golitsyn during the second campaign in Crimea may indicate a love affair in the use of such words as *moj svet, batjuška, moja duša*, which have little meaning beyond the epistolary conventions of the day.

According to La Neuville, the alliance between

Golitsyn and the tsarevna was not a purely political one. A recent history of the Romanovs states unequivocally that "in an act of supreme liberation, Sofia took Golitsyn to her bed and made him her lover".[26] In the play, Sofia meets Golitsyn in her private quarters and entices him to her bedchamber, leaving no doubt about their intimacy, which also appears to be her only and most direct strategy in the attempt to impress upon her lover the need to stop Peter by having Shaklovity kill him before the young tsar can destroy them.

But Golitsyn, who praises truth and divine justice, is reluctant to obey the tsarevna's demands and rejects Shaklovity's offer to rid them of Peter. Although he declares his love for Sofia and claims that she is "the empress through whom Russia will move from darkness to the light", Golitsyn does not see the need to protect her by allowing for Peter's murder, in spite of Sofia's misgivings. In the play, his gentle character follows the dictates of recorded history. As pointed out in Patrick Gordon's account, Vasili Golitsyn hesitated when urged by his cousin Boris Golitsyn to come to the Trinity Monastery where Peter was mustering all his supporters and preparing to overthrow the tsarevna by force. Still hoping for an amicable solution at that time, the "mild" Vasili Golitsyn asked his cousin Boris to "be a good instrument and agree the parties".[27]

It seems plausible, in the world of the play, that Vasili

---

[26]W. Bruce Lincoln, *The Romanovs*, London, 1981, 67.

[27]Quoted in Sofia, *Regent of Russia; 1657-1704*, "Overthrown", 257.

Golitsyn is also mildly amused by both Priest Sylvester's earlier warning that evil is childish, impetuous and quarrelsome, whereas good is grown-up, patient and wise, and Shaklovity's fear of the cruel Peter who will torture and kill the *streltsy* by the axe. The tsar, Vasili Golitsyn insists, completely missing out on the irony of his own gullibility, is just "a boy. What can he do? What power does he have? A toy army of two hundred men. And", Golitsyn goes on, in an attempt to alleviate Shaklovity's fear, "do not forget. We are not villains, we are not conspirators. We are the law. We are the state". Earlier in the play, which carefully calibrates the two Golitsyns' dramatically opposing views, Boris Golitsyn also emphasises the need to have law, but of a very different kind from Vasili's idealistic concept. Boris's proclamation that "law must be like iron", triggers his ward Peter's enthusiastic support for what later, in the Soviet Union, became a single infallible law that ignored and deceived millions of people in the name of a unifying, national cause that precluded then, as in Tsar Peter's case, the energetic pursuit of autocratic self-interest:

> I love law and order. Everything orderly! Everything like it's supposed to be! Everything in its proper place! Houses all in a neat row, everything inside the houses in regulation order, clothes, work, play all by the book, everything! And no idle thoughts in people's heads, but only one cause. The national cause.

As the play unfolds beyond Vasili Golitsyn's Neverland fantasy of trusting the law and the state to do what is right, the young Peter is the very embodiment of a childish man who mocks the court and indulges in puerile and cruel pursuits under Boris Golitsyn's care. The first outburst of Peter's disdain for Golitsyn is triggered in the play by the herald's proclamation of the boyar's great deeds in the second Crimean expedition, which the real-life Peter had refused to treat as a victory. The eulogistic tone of the play that exalts Golitsyn and his heroic exploits – "the commander-in-chief advanced on Perekop where our glorious army made the Khan and the godless Tatars tremble in dread" – duplicates on stage the elaborate ceremony which the tsarevna organized at the Kremlin. According to documents of the time, she welcomed "our own boyar [with] gracious thanks for your great and devoted service. By your efforts those savage and inveterate foes of the Holy Cross and all Christendom have been crushed and defeated and scattered by our royal armies in their infidel abode".[28]

Peter's refusal in real life to be a part of the ceremonies or to accept the praise and rich gifts which the tsarevna lavishes on Golitsyn finds its corresponding outburst on stage in the young tsar's fury:

I decree nothing of the sort! A reward for what? A hundred thousand soldiers marched to the gates of Crimea, were afraid to join battle, and then went away again. An unheard-of disgrace! The people are talking about it. You should be tried, not rewarded! With the air of a statesman, which only infuriates

[28] *Polnoe sobranie zakonov*, vol. 3, no. 1340, 20.

Tsar Peter all the more, Golitsyn points out that one must look further than the mere search for immediate glory; in fact, his questions strike a chord that resonates with today's audience. "What business did we have in Crimea? . . . What would have been the point of a large-scale war"?

Peter's verbal and physical abuse as he screams at Goltsyn – "How dare you contradict the tsar, you peasant! . . . You climbed into Sonya's bed and now you think you are the tsar! Sonya is not your state! She's not your bitch, so that the whole of Russia . . ." – and later in the play his fury at Shaklovity and the German officer instructing his toy regiment, point in the direction of a controlling and vengeful madman who needs to be thwarted.

In a dramatisation made possible by the play's imagined scenario and its voices both old (from the historical past) and contemporary (from the present of the play), the tsarevna, Golitsyn and Shaklovity bring up both the "what if" and the "foretold future". It looks like they need to act before their fears materialise and Peter's unspeakable cruelty brings the tsarevna's overthrow and confinement, Vasili Golitsyn's exile and the confiscation of all his properties, and Shaklovity's torture and death. Such grim premonitions bring to Shaklovity's mind the fear of living again in a time "like the time of Ivan the Terrible", of the tsarevna being "locked up to the end of her days, wasting away never to be released", and of the *streltsy* being "hanged from the walls of the Kremlin", as famously depicted in Vasily Ivanovich Surikov's (1848-1916) "Morning of the Streltsys' Execution" (1881), at the Tretyakov Gallery in Moscow.

Broadening the framework of the conversation, Vasili Golitsyn's imaginary bodyguard and teller of "rambling stories" from his days spent prospecting for gold, Tryokhglazov, adds to the frisson of atrocities the image of the multitudes of Siberian snakes that had to be killed in infancy, before their fangs filled with venom and they bit all the horses. In all its crudity, which makes the allusion to Tsar Peter quite obvious, Tryokhglazov's story triggers Vasili Golitsyn's remark that "a human being, and even less so a tsar, is not a serpent". In agreement with the tsarevna and Shaklovity, Tryokglazov is quick to point out that "a human being, and even more so a tsar, is far more dangerous than a serpent".

At this point, in the play's "what if" scenario, Golitsyn relents and allows Shaklovity to dispatch Tryokhglazov to Preobrazhensky to murder Tsar Peter, the snake under whose rule Russia could never be beautiful, could never achieve the prosperity Golitsyn dreams of achieving. As young Peter and Boris Golitsyn play with a ship's wheel, Tryokhglazov murders the tsar allowing for the tsarevna's reign and Vasili Golitsyn's enlightened leadership.

Recorded history, however, brings back on stage the moment in which Tryokhglazov rushes in to kill young Peter. This time, Tryokhglazov announces that the *streltsy*, led by Shaklovity, are on their way to kill

Peter. As the young tsar is whisked away to the Trinity Monastery, where he will eventually be joined by most of the court's boyars, the play nears its foregone conclusion. Boris tells Peter that he will be great and will build a great city . . . Once again, the play interrogates Russia's history in a subtle confrontation with the present. Was Tsar Peter's celebrated creation of St. Petersburg on the marshes a use of forced-labour similar to that employed by Stalin when he built Magnitogorsk, with just as much human sacrifice, on the deserted steppe?

The Regent Sofia was clearly a complex character and ruler, not just a precursor of Tsar Peter. Determined and capable, she has nevertheless been treated rather unfairly by biographers and historians. A portrait like Ilya Repin's (1844-1930) 1879 "Princess Sofia Alexeyevna a Year after her Incarceration in the Novodevichy Convent 1698, during the Execution of the Streltsy and the Torturing of all her Servants" at the Tretyakov Gallery gives enough information for her biographer Henry Troyat's description of the tsarevna as "massive and terrible", "this fat shapeless woman with the domineering look in her eye",[29] and so on.

Inasmuch as there seems to have been little or no interest in her personality, Akunin's play leaves a sense of nostalgia for Tsarevna Sofia's unfulfilled potential to rule over a better Russia, and of sadness for her life wasted within the confines of a monastery.

Ileana Alexandra Orlich

---

[29]Troyat, *Peter the Great*, London 1987, 13, 33.

DRAMATIS PERSONAE
(In Order of Appearance)

PRINCE VASILI (VASYA, VASKA) VASILYEVITCH GOLITSYN: *the head of government, a handsome man of forty-five*

PRINCE BORIS ALEKSEYEVICH GOLITSYN: *the tutor of Tsar Peter, a jolly fellow of thirty-eight*

THE TWO IN BLACK: *the devil knows who they are*

ANIKEY TRYOKHGLAZOV ('THREE EYES'): *a Siberian artisan, a man of advanced age, with a round birthmark in the middle of his forehead*

THE FOOL: *a man whose face is a gurning mask*

THE BEAR: *knows how to dance and drink vodka*

A FLUTE PLAYER

THE CAPTAIN OF THE PUBLIC WATCH: *a timeless character: the upholder of law and order*

FOY DE LA NEUVILLE: *a timeless character: the enraptured foreigner*

COURT PRIEST SYLVESTER MEDVEDEV: *a timeless character: the Russian sage*

PRINCESS SOFIA (SONYA): *an unattractive woman, past the first flush of youth*

TSAR PETER (PETRUSHA, PETYA, PETENKA): *a difficult youth*

TSAR IVAN ALEKSEYEVITCH: *a young man with developmental difficulties*

JACK: *a timeless character: the butler*

FYODOR LEONTYEVITCH SHAKLOVITY: *head of the Streltsy Department, man of action*

THE DOWAGER TSARINA NATALYA KIRILLOVNA: *an anxious lady of anxious age*

TSARINA YEVDOKIYA: *a very young woman, who looks like she is asleep*

DRUNKS, GUARDS, CLOWNS

The play is set in Moscow and its outskirts

ACT 1
SCENE 1

(*A drinking establishment in Moscow. At the edge of the stage, with their backs turned to the audience, sit two men wearing long, shabby hooded capes. There are other tables too, at one of which sits a man in a blue kaftan, eating slowly. On the table in front of him a long knout lies coiled. Next to the man in blue, but not with him, sits a man fidgeting. At another table two dour men sit shoulder to shoulder. They drink wine, whispering to each other at intervals. An indistinct thrum of voices and drunken laughter can be heard. Individual cries can be made out, whose meaning is unintelligible: "Och, the fever! The scaly wee crake!", "Hoy, thou! Thou suck'st it doon, ne'er tirest of sucking!" "Ach, corking! Ach, soared with the gyrfalcon!" "I'm tight, Christian brothers, like a bustard!")*

(*The two men sitting at the front of the stage, start talking, turning to each other, but still with their backs to the audience.*)

FIRST MAN: For as it is written in the estimable *Testament of Basileus Caesar to his Son Leo Philosophus,*

"Every right-thinking man must measure himself by a strict measure, lest another speak idly of him with evil words". And further in this wise: "Each man in possession of a mind must study how to flee the vain sagacity of human sagaciousness and avoid the stumbling blocks of dubious charms . . ."

SECOND MAN: Oft is it writ in this wise, brother most sagacious: "To every utterance the proper time and the proper place". A tavern is not the place for ornate dictums, but for drinking.

(Little by little the dialogue becomes comprehensible. The din of the tavern customers also becomes comprehensible. At intervals their conversations are interrupted by cries of, "Pour me another!" "Good health to all!" "It's you who are the goat!")

FIRST MAN: You're right.

(Turning around, he slowly looks at the faces of the audience.)

FIRST MAN: A lot of common folk here in the tavern. More than in church. Look at the mugs on them! They're staring . . . What's this you've brought me, Boris? You know I don't drink wine . . .

SECOND MAN: But you love the common folk. You're always lamenting over them. Just take a closer look at them. You'll find it instructive.

FIRST MAN: These aren't the common folk. They're layabouts, tavern drunkards.

SECOND MAN: No, Vasya, these are the common folk. When you see them from the window of your carriage, they bow. In church they pretend to be pious, but in the wild, left to themselves, this is what they're like. Take a good look. What, don't you like the Orthodox folk? They're still good-humoured, even when drunk. God forbid you see them angry.

FIRST MAN: (*about to stand up*) Let's go. I haven't got time to sit around in dumps like this.

SECOND MAN: (*holding him back*) Wait a minute. This is no mere tavern, but a bona fide dive. In just a moment you'll understand why I brought you here. You won't regret it. Look, here they are!
> (*The sound of a flute. Enter THE FOOL, wearing a hideous, mocking mask. He carries a bag slung over one shoulder and leads THE BEAR on a chain. THE FLUTE PLAYER comes dancing behind.*)

FOOL: Och, my dropwort ceiling beams,
Och, tawny-jamb windowsills,
Ach, my gullied hearthstone,
Ach, my mad, perforated bonce!

We nabbed carp with wee bristles,

We hooked ladies' nightshirts!
We caught whatever we could grab,
Scoff it down, kitties, no holds barred!
> (*THE FOOL goes to the front of the stage and in the following addresses the audience directly. His ditties become more and more intelligible, the manner of his performance gradually becomes contemporary, so that by the end it's almost like rapping.*)

FOOL: Let me give it to you straight, Christian brothers,
And once you're in on it, you're going to laugh
At how Mother Russia's getting along
And the crazy things going down round here.

Maybe we're off our heads with booze,
Maybe it's a bad case of the DTs,
But look up there – Holy Mother of God!
Rooshia's gone all cross-eyed!

It's as if two suns shone in the sky,
It's as if two moons silvered the night,
We've got two Tsars Alekseyevitch,
The one weirder than the other.
> (*He takes off his mask and puts his fool's cap on THE BEAR. He takes a doll out of his bag. THE BEAR begins to swing it, clownishly mimicking Tsar Ivan.*)

FOOL: Here's the eldest: Ivan Alekseyevitch.
God's little birdie, a childlike soul.
He's able to sit in the golden room.

But as he's sick, he plays with dolls there.
>   (*He puts a tatty European-style tricorn hat on THE*
>   *BEAR. THE FLUTE PLAYER beats a tambourine like*
>   *a drum. THE BEAR marches back and forth.*)

FOOL: Here's the younger: Peter Alekseyevitch.
It's not dolls, but soldiers he's into.
He's all jumpy, got the falling sickness,
Got a bent for German sort of stuff.
>   (*THE BEAR jerks, as if having a spasm, and the tricorn*
>   *hat falls off. THE FIDGETY MAN sitting next to THE*
>   *MAN IN THE BLUE KAFTAN stands up and silently*
>   *leaves. THE FOOL puts a woman's headdress on THE*
>   *BEAR, who begins to mimic the Princess Sofia.*)

FOOL: And with mighty tsars like these, Old Russia
Found herself in a strange situation
An old bag now rules the Rooshian state,
Bitch Sonya, the Muscovite princess.
>   (*THE FIRST MAN rises angrily to his feet. THE*
>   *SECOND MAN grabs him by his sleeve.*)

SECOND MAN: Listen, listen. The rest will be more
interesting.

FOOL: Bitch Sonya, the Muscovite princess,
Burly, shameless old bag that she is,
She canoodles with Vasya Golitsyn,
The saviour of this nation of ours.

(THE FOOL starts hugging and kissing THE BEAR. Laughter in the tavern. THE FOOL does the rounds of the tavern tables with his cap. THE MAN IN THE BLUE KAFTAN tosses a coin in the cap. THE SECOND MAN pours wine into a mug, proffers it. THE FOOL accepts it with a nod, takes a sip, and then gives it to THE BEAR to drink. THE BEAR also gives a bow. THE FOOL puts on a cardboard helmet and takes up a cardboard sword, brandishing it menacingly. THE BEAR waves its paw at him, as if he were going off to war.)

FOOL: Off to war the heroic Vaska goes.
He wants to conquer the Crimea.
But when he got there, they kicked his arse,
And he ran blubbing all the way home.
> *(THE FLUTE PLAYER knocks THE FOOL off his feet and kicks him in the rump. THE FOOL drops his helmet and sword, crawls on all fours, and with tears in his eyes rushes into the arms of THE BEAR, who pats him to comfort him. The laughter grows even louder.)*

SECOND MAN: Well, how do you like it?
> *(The public guard burst in: THE CAPTAIN and three STRELTSY. THE FIDGETER is with them.)*

CAPTAIN: State business! Arrest the clowns, lads!
> *(One of the STRELTSY grabs THE FOOL, another THE FLUTE PLAYER. The third moves toward THE BEAR, who growls menacingly.)*

CAPTAIN: Cut down whoever resists. That was the order.
(The STRELETS draws his sword. THE BEAR drops to all fours and runs off. THE CAPTAIN paces menacingly around the tavern. He comes to a stop in front of the audience.)

CAPTAIN: Look at how many of you there are, but only a single honest man among you to report these insults to the authorities. Look at me, you cabbage! I'll chop you and bake you in a pie.

FIRST MAN: Listen, let them go.

SECOND MAN: Are you joking? They made a mockery of the authorities, insulted the rulers. They cut out your tongue for that.

FIRST MAN: A bad law, a stupid law. I tried to repeal it, but the boyars voted against me.
(Just as menacingly, the CAPTAIN paces toward the back of the stage, among the tables. The STRELTSY start binding the hands of the arrested men.)

SECOND MAN: The boyars were right to vote against it. The common folk should treat the authorities with the same respect as their own mothers. From mockery it's a short road to rebellion.

FIRST MAN: A long road. Better to let them chatter and mock. Better to release the fools.

SECOND MAN: Well then. It wasn't me they mocked.
   (*Goes over to THE CAPTAIN*)

SECOND MAN: Hey, chief! Give the order to untie them.

CAPTAIN: And who are you to give orders?
   (*THE SECOND MAN takes off his hooded cape, beneath which is a rich kaftan.*)

SECOND MAN: I am Prince Boris Golitsyn, a boyar close to Tsar Peter Alekseyevitch. Heard of me?

CAPTAIN: (*with a bow*) Of course I have! Don't take it amiss, boyar, but in this affair, you have no authority over me. This was an insult to both their royal majesties, the great sovereign Sofia Alexeyevitch and the glorious Prince Vasili Vasilyevitch, the helmsman of the affairs of state.

BORIS GOLITSYN: (*to the first man*) Step up, illustrious man. As you can see, Tsar Peter's boyars are not held in esteem by your grabbers.

FIRST MAN: (*also stands up and doffs his hooded cape, his garb is richer still, and around his neck he wears a gold chain*) It is I, Vasili Golitsyn. Do as my cousin Boris

Alekseyevitch says. Unbind the fools, release them. Let their bear be confined, lest it scare somebody in the street to death.

(*All those seated rise to their feet, doff their caps, make low bows. The guards bow too.*)

VASILI GOLITSYN: (*turns to the audience, frowns, waves his hand*) All right, all right, you don't have to stand up too. And another thing: either don't laugh or don't bow . . . Let's go, Boris. We've had our fun.

(*Exeunt the GOLITSYNS. THE TWO IN BLACK move to the front of the stage and the curtain comes down behind them.*)

SCENE 2

BORIS GOLITSYN: What, Vasya, you are offended? Did you see how they were griping about your Crimean campaign?

VASILI GOLITSYN: Fools! They ought to be glad that it turned out without great bloodshed and that I brought the men back alive. They don't understand . . .

BORIS GOLITSYN: Perhaps it is you who do not understand them. What, in your opinion, is a Russian man?

VASILI GOLITSYN: A man is a man. When things go well for him, he's good. When things go badly, he's bad.

BORIS GOLITSYN: Wrong, Brother. You're mistaken. What is the most important thing in a Russian man?

VASILI GOLITSYN: What?

BORIS GOLITSYN: He is a Russian first and foremost, and only secondarily a man.

VASILI GOLITSYN: Really?

BORIS GOLITSYN: Really. Take yourself: Who are you? I mean you in the most precise and succinct sense, whereby you can't be mistaken for anybody else.

VASILI GOLITSYN: (*ponders*) Who am I? I am Vasili Golitsyn.

BORIS GOLITSYN: Correct. There are a lot of people in the world, but only one Vasili Golitsyn. It's the same with nations. Every people has its own character, its own customs, its own fate. And while one prospers, another perishes.

VASILI GOLITSYN: Be that as it may. And what of the Russian people?

BORIS GOLITSYN: It is like the fool's pet bear. Underfeed it and it will grow surly. Overfeed it and it will grow stubborn and cease to dance to your flute. There are four rules. The bear will follow whomever adheres to them. The first rule: feed it, but not to satiety. The second: play an intricate tune on your flute, so that it will want to dance. The third: let it drink a little wine now and then, to soothe its soul. And the final rule, the most unrelenting of all: What do you think it is?

VASILI GOLITSYN: What is it?

BORIS GOLITSYN: Keep the bear on a strong chain.

VASILI GOLITSYN: How about we drop the metaphors? I know what you and your Naryshkins in the Preobrazhensky Regiment are dreaming of: how to depose the regent Sofia and seize hold of the state. Let's imagine you pull it off. You depose, you seize, and then what? Just take a look at our Russia. Ignorance, thievery, savagery. A hundred years behind Europe. No matter how much I heave, no matter how hard I pull, the cart creaks and barely budges.

BORIS GOLITSYN: That's because you harness yourself to the cart rather than a horse. Let me tell you what we'll do when my ward Petrusha becomes a true autocrat. Russians are not Romans; they don't require much bread or many circuses. But they do need a great aim, and we shall give them one. Rather than a flute to whose merry tune they might dance. A great aim is a chain. A stout one. Our nation is great, it can move mountains, if it is guided wisely. You call us backward? No problem, we'll catch up. From Europe we'll adopt what is beneficial and reject what is harmful.

VASILI GOLITSYN: And what is harmful in Europe?

BORIS GOLITSYN: Neither their aim nor their chain. Because over there everything is all over the place. Everybody thinks whatever he likes. He goes wherever he wants. But over here there will be a single will: the state's. And a single mind.

VASILI GOLITSYN: Of what kind?

BORIS GOLITSYN: Of greatness. Taken in himself, a man is petty, self-seeking, he snuffles around on the ground looking for food, like a mouse. But when men come together, united as a nation, they become great. This is why rule is required; this is why the state is required.

VASILI GOLITSYN: But I think the state is needed for something else: in order that people might live better. A country's greatness resides in the happiness of its inhabitants.

BORIS GOLITSYN: Wake up, Vasya! This is Russia, not Holland. That sort of thing has never existed here, and it never will. You're clever, cleverer than any of us, but you've got your head in the clouds. Let's build what can be built down here on the ground, not castles in the sky.

VASILI GOLITSYN: Even without you I know what I'm not going to build: something that will do as long as it has one or two floors. I will build solidly and leave a blueprint for the future. It will be easier for the builders then. One day, the building will soar to the sky. And life in it will be happier than it is today.

BORIS GOLITSYN: Verily is it written: no ruler more dangerous than the dreamer. But why do you think that people should live happily? In which of the Gospels is it written? Man must fulfil his purpose and endure suffering without complaint. Ask the Patriarch or whomever you wish. Here in Russia, greatness lies not in happiness, but happiness in greatness. If everybody started caring about his own personal happiness, what would become of Russia?

VASILI GOLITSYN: So, this is how you're educating Peter. And what about him, is he going along with it?

BORIS GOLITSYN: There's no telling what goes on in that head of his. He's still green, unpredictable, you never know which way he's going to turn. And he's got a violent temper, too: he sometimes scares even me. But that's the kind of autocrat the Russian mare needs. Peter is growing up. He'll harness the mare; he'll wield the whip to make her gallop. You don't frequent the Preobrazhensky, but it's mayhem there, every day some new scheme.

VASILI GOLITSYN: So I've heard. Tsar Peter plays at funny soldiers, plays at building funny ships, dances German dances.

BORIS GOLITSYN: You know nothing. While you and your Sofia have been canoodling and composing sagacious treatises, Peter has grown up. He is now a married man. By law and by custom he should be ruling already, but instead our ruler is a girl. How long will this go on? Think about it, Vasya. The two of you are going to have to give up power, and then where are you going to hide? Better you do so willingly. We're cousins, both of us are Golitsyns. I'll look after you. I won't let you perish.

VASILI GOLITSYN: Thank you, brother, both for the advice and for taking me to the performance. This is what I think: Was it you who hired those jesters?

BORIS GOLITSYN: Did I hire the audience to laugh at you too?

VASILI GOLITSYN: They found your Peter amusing as well.

BORIS GOLITSYN: No matter. They won't for long. When we come to power, we won't let jesters like them get away with it. We'll string them up in public, alongside their bear. As a warning. So that the common folk will see and be afraid.

VASILI GOLITSYN: And then there will be greatness? Everybody will be afraid, everybody silent, but Russia will be great?

BORIS GOLITSYN: Tell me, Vasya: is God great? But the people are afraid of Him and dare not blaspheme Him. It should be the same in the state, otherwise your tower to the sky will come crashing down like Babel.
  (*VASILI GOLITSYN produces a large pocket watch. He opens the lid. The clock chimes and plays a tune.*)

VASILI GOLITSYN: Time for me to go. I'm due to receive the French ambassador.

BORIS GOLITSYN: Is that German? A clever invention. But no matter, we'll catch up with Europe and then we'll have our own Russian pocket watches.

VASILI GOLITSYN: No, you'll still have to buy German ones. Men who are afraid don't do much inventing . . . Farewell, Boris. Time will tell which of us is right. Damn it, will you cut it out already?
(*He tries to stop the incessant music from the watch.*)

BORIS GOLITSYN: Is it time? Hardly.
(*BORIS GOLITSYN exits.*)
(*VASILI GOLITSYN shakes his watch. It has jammed.*)

VASILI GOLITSYN: Quiet, you German piece of junk!
(*TWO FIGURES IN BLACK emerge from the shadows. They creep toward the prince. One of them is holding a knife. VASILI GOLITSYN abruptly turns around. He leaps back. He drops the watch and it finally falls silent.*)

FIRST MAN IN BLACK: Got you, scurvy devil!

SECOND MAN IN BLACK: Our prayers are answered! He's caught!
(*THE FIRST MAN IN BLACK lunges, but the prince dodges the blow. He reaches for the sword at his side, but does not have time to draw, because THE SECOND MAN IN BLACK rushes at him with a knife. GOLITSYN is caught between two foes.*)

FIRST MAN IN BLACK: You won't escape!

SECOND MAN IN BLACK: You'll breathe your last! (*From behind appears a man in a blue kaftan, wielding a long whip. THE MAN IN BLUE strikes out with his whip, catching THE FIRST MAN IN BLACK around the neck, he jerks him toward him and stabs him with a dagger. THE FIRST MAN IN BLACK falls. THE SECOND MAN IN BLACK hurls himself at GOLITSYN, but the MAN IN BLUE throws his dagger at the assassin's back. He falls.*)

MAN IN BLUE: Are you hurt?

VASILI GOLITSYN: (*feeling himself*) It would seem not. Where did they spring out from?

MAN IN BLUE: They followed you, waited till you were alone. Who are they?

VASILI GOLITSYN: (*casts an uninterested glance at the bodies*) The Devil knows. Could be anyone. Many are those who try for my life. Last winter, a knifeman jumped right inside my sleigh. In the Crimea, somebody shot at the tent in which I was sleeping. Better you tell me who you are, good fellow. Had it not been for you, I would be lying dead by now.

MAN IN BLUE: I am Anikey Tryokhglazov, the Siberian artisan.

VASILI GOLITSYN: And what is your trade?

MAN IN BLUE: The usual, for Siberia. I went there for sables. Trapped a great many. Then I started to prospect for gold. Haven't found any yet.

VASILI GOLITSYN: Who tells you which to go looking for there, sables or gold?

TRYOKHGLAZOV: (*shrugs*) Who tells anybody what to do in Siberia? I decide for myself.

VASILI GOLITSYN: What do you mean, for yourself?
    (*TRYOKHGLAZOV shrugs once more.*)

VASILI GOLITSYN: This is the first time I've seen a man in Russia who decides for himself how to live. What's more, I am a stranger to you, but you came to my aid against the knifemen. By yourself. Few men are capable of this.

TRYOKHGLAZOV: (*scratches the back of his head*) I ought to lie to you, but I won't. I know who you are. I was sitting in the tavern. I've come to Moscow from Siberia with a petition. I go knocking on official doors, I hand out bribes, but I've got nowhere. I'd started to think I'd have to go back empty-handed. But then all of a sudden none other than the tsar's tutor, Prince Golitsyn himself! I followed you, wracking my brains as to how I might approach you. And then a stroke of luck.

VASILI GOLITSYN: You're forthright. I like that.

TRYOKHGLAZOV: What are you doing, walking alone? When the whole state depends on a single man, to stroll around without guards isn't brave, it's . . .

VASILI GOLITSYN: . . . Stupid? That's what she says too, all the time. But I don't like it when somebody is tramping alongside me; I can't hear my own thoughts. Come with me, artisan. I have to go home. On the way, you can tell me what this petition of yours is all about.

TRYOKHGLAZOV: (*points at the bodies*) What about them? We should wait for the public guard to arrive.

VASILI GOLITSYN: They come running only if there's been a denunciation. You can wait all you like for them if there's been a robbery or a murder. Let's go, Anikey. I'm in a hurry.
   (*Exeunt.*)
   (*BEGGARS emerge to rob the dead bodies. They squabble over the loot, then drag the corpses out by the legs.*)

VASILI GOLITSYN: (*from offstage*) What is it like in Siberia?

TRYOKHGLAZOV: It's good.

SCENE 3

(An office in the palace of Vasili Golitsyn. The whole of the rear wall is covered by a bookcase. A large globe rests on a stand. European-style paintings on the wall.)
(Enter VASILI GOLITSYN and TRYOKHGLAZOV.)

VASILI GOLITSYN: Why do you want to sell your stake-holding on the Amur River?

TRYOKHGLAZOV: There's no gold on our side, but they say there's a lot on the other side. And nobody pans for gold. The governor doesn't allow it. It's forbidden, he says. That's why I've come to Moscow, to get an official letter. I go from one government office to the next. All the officials make promises. They all pocket a bribe, but after that, nothing. Maybe you can help. There's none higher than you.

VASILI GOLITSYN: I will not help you. The Amur governor is right to forbid it. It is the land of the Chinese god emperor. We dare not quarrel with him. And so, you have travelled the length of Russia in vain. But it was not in vain that you met me. Those officials would have strung you along for a long time. They weren't telling you the truth. What am I to do with them, the idle brood? As the saying goes, you can't live with them, but you can't live without them.

TRYOKHGLAZOV: Damn! It took me a year to get here, and it'll take a year to get back. With nothing to show for it . . .

VASILI GOLITSYN: Before the ambassador arrives, tell me about yourself. I can see that you are not stupid, you are strong, you live by your wits. What kind of man are you?

TRYOKHGLAZOV: I'm a man in and of myself, separate and alone. I live my life like water.

VASILI GOLITSYN: What do you mean by that?

TRYOKHGLAZOV: Water is strongest of all. Nothing can conquer it, nothing can destroy it. Where it can flow, it flows. It makes its way around every obstacle. When the winter frost sets in, it freezes. When fire blazes, it rises to the sky as steam. Where it finds a suitable spot, it falls as rain. Such a man am I.

VASILI GOLITSYN: You are a philosopher. A philosopher who is good in a fight is rare indeed. And you're not over-talkative. You do not hold forth unless you are asked . . . Listen, Anikey, why go back to Siberia, if you haven't obtained your official letter? Remain here with me. I could do with a bodyguard like you. I often have to go places, sometimes in secret. Be my shadow. See that nobody sticks a knife in my back. Serve me. It will be to your advantage. Afterward, I'll send you to Siberia to be a governor yourself . . . Don't you have anything to say?

TRYOKHGLAZOV: I'm thinking.

VOICE: (*from offstage*) The royal ambassador Monsieur Foy de la Neuville entreats admittance to the prince!

VASILI GOLITSYN: Remain here. I'll see whether you know how to be a shadow.
 (*TRYOKHGLAZOV withdraws into a corner. Enter NEUVILLE. He bows so low that his long wig brushes the floor. VASILI GOLITSYN goes to greet him.*)

NEUVILLE: (*still in a bowing position*) Mihi est honor magnus in domo tuo esse, domine!

VASILI GOLITSYN: Et mihi est voluptas cum visitore tam illustrato disputare. Asside in sedem, legate honeste.
 (*VASILI cordially clasps the ambassador by the shoulders, guides him to a chair, and then sits down. Hereinafter the audience will not be further tortured with Latin.*)

VASILI GOLITSYN: Monsieur ambassador, during my

audience with the ruling princess, I promised to answer all your questions in private conference. Please do not hesitate to ask.

NEUVILLE: First of all, let me convey once again His Majesty's heartfelt gratitude for the Crimean expedition. It was a brilliant operation! You have helped us so greatly! Thanks to Russia, the khan was unable to attack Poland and the Sultan was fearful to deploy his fleet in the Mediterranean.

VASILI GOLITSYN: The main thing is that the Turks and the Tatars know that the Russian army is intact and able to return at any time. In politics, the hand raised to strike a blow is more important than the blow itself. But if I am not mistaken, it was not about war that you wished to talk to me.

NEUVILLE: That is right, my lord, I wish to ask you about Russia. In Europe, they are saying wonderful things about the Russian prince protector's innovations and grand plans. Tell me, are these tidings true?

VASILI GOLITSYN: What have we done that Europe finds so surprising?

NEUVILLE: (*consults a notebook*) Is it true that you have passed lenient laws? That, unlike us, you no longer apply the death penalty for theft?

VASILI GOLITSYN: It's true. For a first offence, we only cut off the thief's ears.

NEUVILLE: Unheard-of leniency! And is it true that you no longer bury women alive for murdering their husbands?

VASILI GOLITSYN: Yes. Now, we merely cut off their heads.

NEUVILLE: It's enlightened; it's European! I have also been told, although I do not know whether to believe it, that orphaned children are no longer liable to payment of their parents' debts if there is no inheritance. But this goes against the laws of commerce! The lender must bear the loss.

VASILI GOLITSYN: The lender bears no loss. The treasury pays off the deceased's debt. That is why we have a state, so that children will not be legally liable for a feckless father.

NEUVILLE: And is it true that criminals sentenced to hard labour may now take their families with them into exile? Where is the penal severity in this?

VASILI GOLITSYN: The meaning of judicial retribution lies not in punishment but in correction. A man who has not been separated from his family is less inclined to repeat his wrongdoing, and his children are not reduced to becoming beggars or pickpockets.

NEUVILLE: Amazing! What is more, here in Moscow I have seen special guards on the streets, who shout at the coachmen to drive this way and not that. Why so?

VASILI GOLITSYN: So that the carts and waggons won't collide. Everybody must keep to the right, with those coming from the opposite direction passing on their left. Long horsewhips have been outlawed, because the carters accidentally used to hit passers-by with them, which caused constant public affray. The carters are also required to collect their horses' manure from the road. By order, those on foot must keep out of the middle of the road and instead walk at the side, by the fence.

NEUVILLE: (*jots it down in his notebook*) Amazing, amazing . . . Such great, such unheard-of reforms!

VASILI GOLITSYN: (*becoming more and more animated*) We haven't got to the reforms yet. Just wait till we get to the reforms. Here I have an extensive treatise, which I have compiled: *On Civil Life, or On Improvement of All Matters Pertaining to the Common People.*
   (*He takes a voluminous manuscript from the desk.*)
Herein are listed all the things that need to be done in order to achieve a thriving Russian state. Above all

else, the peasants need to be emancipated from serf-
dom, because good citizens cannot come from slaves.
Let every man plough his own land, but also pay the
treasury a tax according to his means. I calculate that
this measure will result in a doubling of the state's rev-
enues. We will create a regular army. There are count-
less idlers and restless troublemakers in the land. Rather
than stealing and roaming the highways armed with
clubs, better they serve their country. We will invite the
children of the nobility to attend schools. A modern
state is impossible without an educated class. The eigh-
teenth century is just around the corner, after all. We
will establish embassies in every foreign capital. When
neighbours get along with each other, there are fewer
wars and trade is more profitable. We will rebuild our
wooden cities in stone, to prevent them from burning
to the ground whenever there is a hot dry summer. We
will forbid persecution of those of other faiths. There
are many ethnic groups in our state; let nobody feel
himself a foreigner in Russia. . . . Have you managed to
write it all down?

   (*GOLITSYN takes out his pocket watch, which again
   starts to chime and play a tune. The prince shakes the
   watch.*)

NEUVILLE: (*rising to his feet*) I thank your highness
for granting me your time. Your plans are grandiose!
Incroyables! I wish to write a book about how Russia
will stun the world.

VASILI GOLITSYN: Better you write it in the newspaper. We ourselves are also going to establish newspapers. Once more people have learned to read.

(*Exit the ambassador, bowing.*)

VASILI GOLITSYN: (*to TRYOKHGLAZOV*) Well, what do you think of the ambassador? Will he distort what I told him?

(*TRYOKHGLAZOV comes forward. He takes the pocket watch from the prince, does something to it. The tune stops playing.*)

TRYOKHGLAZOV: I don't think anything about the ambassador. I'm thinking about what you said.

VASILI GOLITSYN: (*surprised*) You understand Latin?

TRYOKHGLAZOV: I haven't roamed the taiga my whole life.

VASILI GOLITSYN: Who then were you before that?

TRYOKHGLAZOV: It doesn't matter who I was. What matters is who I will be: your shadow. Wherever you go, I will be there too. When I am around, nobody will creep up on you from behind.

VASILI GOLITSYN: Why were you undecided earlier, but now you are all of a sudden convinced?

TRYOKHGLAZOV: Certainly not for the sake of a governorship. What use would it be to me? If you are to accomplish even half, even a quarter of what you were talking about just now, you're going to have to have somebody to guard you. Russia needs you.

VASILI GOLITSYN: Oho, now you've started talking about Russia. What happened to, "I live for my own sake, separate and alone. As free as water"?

TRYOKHGLAZOV: If the river is broad and flows in the right direction, why not flow with it? But will you be able to carry such a burden, Prince? Here, it is bravery more than intelligence that is needed.

VASILI GOLITSYN: I have never been a coward. I have led armies into battle and fought hand-to-hand with both the Tatars and the Poles.

TRYOKHGLAZOV: We have no shortage of people brave enough to fight hand-to hand. I'm talking about a different kind of courage . . . But anyway, I'll see.

VASILI GOLITSYN: Yes, you'll see. It's not for nothing that you're called "Three-eyed". . . . I'm tired. I'm going to bed.

TRYOKHGLAZOV: I'll be keeping watch by the door.
    (*Enter the priest SYLVESTER MEDVEDEV. His gait*

*is restive and not at all priestly. His cassock is lilac, his
beard Chekhov-like, and he wears large round spectacles.*)

SYLVESTER: Vasili Vasilyevich, here I am! Can you
believe it? I had supped, said my prayers, and was thinking of going to bed when all of a sudden inspiration
struck! The lines of poetry flowed of themselves. It was
like gathering moonbeams. Here it is: listen.
    (*Produces a piece of paper*)

VASILI GOLITSYN: Greetings, my dear Sylvester. (*To
TRYOKHGLAZOV*) This is Sylvester Medvedev, a man
dear to me. I want you always to give him access to me.
He pops up whenever he likes, unannounced. Like you,
Sylvester is a philosopher. He is also a poet.

SYLVESTER: (*To TRYOKHGLAZOV*) You are a philosopher? Which school? Greek, Latin, German, or French?

TRYOKHGLAZOV: Russian.
    (*He withdraws to a corner of the room*)

VASILI GOLITSYN: Don't mind him, Sylvester. He's
my shadow. Feel at ease. Would you like some wine?

SYLVESTER: It is forbidden to drink wine during the
fast before the Assumption. Unless it is for the sake of
inspiration? But no, first listen to the poem.
    (*He raises his hand and recites*)

Oh, wonders of our omnipotent God,
How blessèd and bounteous are His ways!
What splendour when th'airy pellucidity
Of that world doth nourish the souls of men!
Flee the mendacious clouds of providence
And thou shalt take comfort in the heart's hope.
Glean thou gnosis from wisdom's jealous guards
And thou shalt reckon numbers numberless.
Will then unrest and obscurantism come
If the people are robust in spirit?
From wind-smashed insolence perisheth he
Who from this truth openeth his eyes.
  (*Sylvester's voice cracks, he lifts his spectacles and wipes
  away his tears.*)
What do you think?

VASILI GOLITSYN: Good. But Ovid's original is shorter. And clearer.

SYLVESTER: Would that you understood poetry, Prince! The Latin language is dry and concise precisely because it is dead. But the Russian language is alive; its beauty lies in its exuberance, its verbal excess. It walks in circles, seemingly engaged in pointless and not always intelligible chatter, but Russian poetry is not aimed at a meaning, rather it is addressed straight to the heart. What would be the point of poetry if everything in it were immediately clear? But just yesterday I wrote a simpler poem, especially for you. Be it illustrious in the midst of a hovel and – that which is not great is beautiful. This will not elevate the soul. Inscribe not your virtues on elegant paper. Ah well, poet, this vain labour! You toil to give your all, but do not gain the love of the crowd. Let it be a parable on the lips of all: Wherefore thy good fortune?

VASILI GOLITSYN: Yes, I often think about that. Those for whom I lay down my life do not love me. Of course, it is not the purpose of my labours that the people should love me. But what is worse, Sylvester, is that, to tell the truth, I myself do not love them. You know, this is how I think: "the people" – and I love the people. But I think of the actual living people, the way they really are, which is not very . . . As opposed to the way they will be some time in the future. The way they ought to be . . . That's what . . . grates on me. It's as if I'm pretending, imagining something that doesn't exist.

SYLVESTER: My son, why would the people care whether or not you love them? You do what your heart and mind dictate, and with that you have acquitted your duty. But do not deceive yourself that you are doing it for the sake of the people. Be honest with yourself.

VASILI GOLITSYN: Then for whose sake, in your opinion, do I strive?

SYLVESTER: For the sake of your own soul. This is what you must do above all else: you must devote yourself to the world, do so to your utmost, do all that it is in your power to do. This is what my poem is about, too.

VASILI GOLITSYN: Then it is my task to cry cock-a-doodle-doo, although dawn has yet to arrive?

SYLVESTER: It is good that you cry cock-a-doodle-doo; dawn will arrive.

VASILI GOLITSYN: Also to know the meaning of Good and Evil, to know what is good, what is evil. Each understands them in his own way. Patriarch Joachim says that to believe in God is good, not to believe is evil. My second cousin Boris Alekseyevich, a man of keen mind, says Good is order, Evil chaos. But on the other hand, the greatest order is in immutability, in death, and only when order is disrupted will there be development.

SYLVESTER: But what about your own opinion? What are Good and Evil?

VASILI GOLITSYN: It's very simple: Good is any action whereby man, the state, life in general become better, and Evil is the opposite.

SYLVESTER: No, my son, it does not work like that. What is better for one person might be worse for another. This holds true for the state in particular.

Good and Evil are indeed simple, but not in the way you think.

VASILI GOLITSYN: Very well, then enlighten me.

SYLVESTER: Evil is childish, Good is grown-up. Herein lies the whole wisdom of the matter.

VASILI GOLITSYN: Another of your paradoxes. You claim that a child, who is pure of soul, is evil?

SYLVESTER: Why not? Look at a small child without being affected by his smallness. He is greedy, selfish, shameless, he acts without a thought for others or the consequences of his actions, he refuses to obey, he knows nothing, understands nothing, he is insensately cruel. Now imagine a man of forty who behaved like this. What would you have to say about him? The damnation of hell. As he grows up, a man ceases to spout nonsense, to sully himself, to swallow all kinds of filth; he thinks before he acts. There are also men who achieve true maturity. Such men are patient and wise, unyielding before the strong, lenient before the weak. This is what it means to be a grown-up; this too is the Good. But the trouble is that many people, the majority in fact, behave childishly until their dying day. All the evil in the world arises from the fact that the world is still a child, my son.

VASILI GOLITSYN: And does the same apply to nations?

SYLVESTER: Of course. There are countries that behave like stupid three-year-olds. There are countries that are like fidgety children. There are countries that are as quarrelsome as impetuous youths. But there are not yet any grown-up countries in the world.

VASILI GOLITSYN: Then what is the meaning of God?

SYLVESTER: The grown-up among the brainless, misbehaved, nasty children . . . But hark . . .
   (*Jumps to his feet*)

SYLVESTER: Something stirs . . . O Lord, a poem! "Oh, dull-witted child, open thine eyes, I beseech thee". No, that's not it. "In vain doth the child boggle at the sorrowful father". I depart, Prince, before my inspiration fades. Farewell.
   (*SYLVESTER moves toward the door, muttering to himself.*)

VASILI GOLITSYN: (*laughs*) I'll lead the way. Otherwise you'll get lost in the corridors again.
   (*Like a shadow, TRYOKHGLAZOV follows the prince.*)

VASILI GOLITSYN: Do not follow me here. I have nothing to fear in my own house.
   (*Exeunt SYLVESTER and GOLITSYN. TRYOKHGLAZOV remains. He looks around the*

office. He goes over to the case, examines the books. Suddenly a creak. One of the bookcases starts to move. TRYOKHGLAZOV conceals himself in an alcove. A FIGURE closely wrapped in a cloak and hood emerges from the secret passage that has opened. Treading softly, the figure enters the room. TRYOKHGLAZOV wields his whip, catches the stranger by the neck, pulls him toward himself. He draws a knife.)

TRYOKHGLAZOV: Who are you? I'll kill you!

SOFIA: Let me go, you ignoramus! It is I, the Princess Sofia Alekseyevna!
(*She throws back her hood. Under her cloak is a brocade dress. TRYOKHGLAZOV releases her, pauses, and then bows.*)

SOFIA: Who are you? Where is Prince Vasili Vasilyevich?

TRYOKHGLAZOV: I am his grace's bodyguard. Anikey Tryokhglazov. The prince will return any moment now.

SOFIA: Vasya has hired a bodyguard? Has he been attacked again? Who was it this time? Speak!

TRYOKHGLAZOV: Two men in black. Armed with knives.

SOFIA: My God, I am beside myself . . . Is he safe?

TRYOKHGLAZOV: He is safe. I was there. I will always be there.

SOFIA: (*goes up to TRYOKHGLAZOV and lays both hands on his shoulders*) Look into my eyes. I am able to gaze deep into people; it is a power I have from God. (*She looks at him in silence*) No, I cannot gaze deep into you. But what I was able to glimpse was sufficient. Never be farther than one pace away, do you hear? Go with him wherever he goes. When he is with me in the bedchamber, you will stand guard outside the door.
  (*TRYOKHGLAZOV nods*)
There is none dearer to me in all Russia, in all the world. For my sake, preserve him.
  (*Enter VASILI GOLITSYN.*)

VASILI GOLITSYN: My dear Sonia! What are you doing here? What is wrong?
  (*SOFIA pushes TRYOKHGLAZOV aside and he withdraws to beside the wall. SOFIA rushes to embrace the GOLITSYN.*)

SOFIA: It was becoming alarming . . . You returned from the campaign almost unawares. In the palace, you were almost always in the company of strangers. And so, I decided to pay a visit to our secret passage. Have you been attacked yet again?

VASILI GOLITSYN: The attack failed. I now have a

bodyguard. I see you have already bored into my Anikey with your eyes. Well, does he pass your test?

SOFIA: If he doesn't, I'll wipe the floor with him . . . My light, my joy, my Vasya! How fearful I was while you were away at war! And just now, in the palace, I was tormented at the thought that I would see you, but would not be able to embrace you, to kiss you.
   (*She kisses him passionately.*)

VASILI GOLITSYN: I have not yet told you everything about affairs in the Crimea. There are matters that the boyars need not know. I thought that once I was alone with you . . .

SOFIA: (*interrupts him with her kisses*) Such matters can wait . . .
   (*VASILI waves at TRYOKHGLAZOV, signalling him to go away. TRYOKHGLAZOV turns his face to the wall, but remains.*)

VASILI GOLITSYN: When we are like this together, I feel like the twofold man-woman in Plato's *Symposium*, with two heads and four arms, mighty, invincible, the envy of the gods . . .

SOFIA: (*with a merry laugh*) No, Vasya, we are not Greek, but Russian. You and I are the bicephalous eagle.

VASILI GOLITSYN: The bicephalous eagle is not Russian, but Byzantine, which is to say, Greek. It came to Russia two centuries ago, in the reign of . . .

SOFIA: Oh, you and your scholarship . . . Remember how you told me about ancient history and Russian history, silly little girl that I was? Oh, how splendid you were! How I gazed at you! I was not thinking about Themistocles or Vladimir Krasno Solnyshko, but about one thing only: Why do we tsar's daughters have to be so unhappy? Why are we doomed to live to our dying day as girls? What evil fate made me be born in the tsar's chamber? What would I not give to live my life with Vasya, or at least for us to be lovers . . . Then I would fear nothing! But what is an ugly creature such as I to a handsome, learned man such as he? Honestly, how did you fall in love with me? I am stupid; I feel ill when I look in the mirror.

VASILI GOLITSYN: You are the best and the most beautiful woman in the world. When I look at you, I behold radiance. In Russia, there has been no woman such as you since Princess Olga, Equal-to-the-Apostles. They will write treatises and compose poems about you. You, a woman who rules a country where women are kept locked up, forbidden to open their mouths. You, the empress through whom Russia will move from darkness to the light. I do not know where you find so much courage. This is the mystery before which I remain speechless . . .

SOFIA: What mystery? My audacity is firstly born of fear. The fear of growing old, an old maid, among crones, jesters and holy fools. Secondly, it comes from love. I would do anything just to be with you. There is very little courage in me. If I were really courageous, I would not skulk, but take you for my husband. Every day and every night we would be together . . .

VASILI GOLITSYN: How could that be? I am only a Golitsyn, but you are of the royal blood . . .

SOFIA: Your stock is older and nobler. You are descended from the great Gedmin, whereas my grandfather is said to have served the Pretender at table. But to the devil with blood lines . . . Never mind. Give it time. We will achieve everything we have planned, and nothing will stand in our way. Once you have gained power, you will be ennobled. Then, we shall get married, and nobody will object. And if anybody does, he will regret it . . . Just a little longer and I will get to this. It is time for you to rise higher. Go to the tsars tomorrow. They will reward you for the Crimean campaign. I have prepared a decree on their behalf, and you will be granted a great honour. Henceforward you will be named not tutor, but ruler, the same as in the reign of Godunov.

VASILI GOLITSYN: Ruler? Is it not rash, since the tsars are still alive?

SOFIA: What kind of tsars are they? The one a simple-ton, the other a nestling.

(*She embraces the prince, kisses him.*)

But let us forget about all of it, even if only for a short while. Come, darling, we shall be alone together, with nobody else.

(*She draws him after her. Exeunt, arm in arm. TRYOKHGLAZOV follows, shadowing them.*)

SCENE 4

(The throne room. From behind the curtain comes solemn, pompous music. trumpets, timpani, a drum. Then, many voices cry in chorus: "Glory to the rulers! Glory to Russia!")

HERALD: *(from behind curtain, reads slowly, monotonously)* For thy plenteous and profitable service to us, that such ferocious and primordial foes of the Holy Cross and all Christendom by thy service hitherto unheard of in our royal army were discomfited and postponing their wonted insolence, succumbing to despair and terror . . .

(The curtain opens. The antiquated speech gradually merges into its translation. Side by side on two thrones sit TSAR IVAN and TSAR PETER, wearing identical ceremonial vestments. IVAN has a wispy beard and his mouth lolls open slightly. PETER is very young and lean. The royal vestments look ridiculous on both of them. Behind PETER and to the side stands BORIS GOLITSYN. In the wings stands VASILI GOLITSYN, wearing gilded armour and striking a pose. On the

opposite side of the stage stands the HERALD, holding the decree.)

HERALD: . . . In not yielding to the provocations of the enemy, you, the prince tutor, did not allow yourself to be lured into drawn-out battles, thereby avoiding unnecessary losses. Affrighted by our army's self-restraint, the khan's horde retreated to Perekop in an impotent fury.

(The HERALD moves to the side of the stage, giving a signal. Tinny throats once more set up a cry of: "Glory to the rulers! Glory to Russia!")

HERALD: And on the twentieth day of May, you, the commander-in-chief, advanced on Perekop, saw that it was strongly fortified, and wisely gave the order to pitch camp, so that Christian souls would not be lost in the pointless bloodshed that the devious infidels had no doubt been planning, since they had readied cannons, pitfalls, sharpened stakes, and mines to tear the Russian army to pieces, and had a less intelligent commander rashly given the order to attack, they would have fallen into the trap, from which . . .

(Getting bogged down in the subordinate clause, he once again gives the signal for the chorus to cry: "Glory to the rulers! Glory to Russia!" As the herald ploughs through the text of the decree, the bored tsars come to life. First of all, IVAN gives a gaping yawn. Then PETER jabs him with his elbow. IVAN looks at his brother in fright. He gives a shudder and then sits still. The restless PETER

starts to fidget. BORIS GALITSYN leans over and whispers in his ear. PETER sits up straight.)

HERALD: . . . from which the Orthodox army fortunately escaped, thanks to your cautious foresight, Prince Guardian.

(IVAN turns his head. He catches a fly. He examines it with great interest, pops it in his mouth, spits it out, pulls a teary face. PETER jabs him in the ribs again.)

HERALD: Looming like a dire cloud at the gateway to the Crimea, our glorious army made the khan and the godless Tatars tremble in dread. Meekly and humbly they began to sue for peace, swearing never again to plague the lands of Russia with their plundering raids.

(He waves his hand. "Glory to the rulers! Glory to Russia!" PETER grows more and more restless: his face is congested with fury; he suffers a spasm. BORIS GOLITSYN lays a comforting hand on his shoulder, but to no avail. IVAN, on the other hand, begins to nod off.)

HERALD: After humiliating and humbling the hostile foreigners, you, Prince Guardian, returned in great glory from your campaign, bringing with you much booty, among which the battle banner of the khan.

(VASILI GOLITSYN gives a signal. From off-stage TRYOKHGLAZOV appears, carrying a limp rag attached to an ordinary-looking stick. VASILI looks at it in puzzlement and then, having given it some thought,

goes ahead and lays the so-called banner at the foot of the throne. The chorus shouts, "Glory to the rulers! Glory to Russia!" more loudly than before. IVAN wakes up; his hat falls off. BORIS GOLITSYN picks up the hat and puts it back on IVAN'S head, briefly leaving PETER unattended.)

HERALD: And for these unprecedented exploits we the great rulers decree that you, the glorious Prince Guardian Vasili Vasilyevich Golitsyn be richly rewarded . . .

PETER: (*jumping to his feet*) I decreed nothing of the sort! A reward for what? A hundred thousand soldiers marched to the gates of the Crimea, were afraid to join battle, and then went away again. An unheard-of disgrace! The people are talking about it. You should be tried, not rewarded!

VASILI GOLITSYN: (*sternly*) The people are benighted. They want nothing but bloody victories, enemy heads, booty. But being a ruler, you must look further than that. What business did we have in the Crimea? You can't hold on to it, and what's there anyway? There's no profit in it, only expense, and what is more, the Turks would have struck at us with all their might. What would have been the point of a large-scale war? Our allies were succoured, the Crimean Tatars were contained, losses were avoided. We achieved everything we set out to achieve . . .

(*PETER is trembling with fury. From behind him, BORIS GOLITSYN signals to the guardian prince: Tone it down.*)

PETER: (*interrupts, his voice rising to a squealing yelp*) Whom do you think you are talking to? How dare you contradict the tsar, you peasant! The nerve of him! You climbed into Sonya's bed and now you think you are the tsar! Sonya is not your state! She's not your bitch so that the whole of Russia . . .
(*The HERALD hastily waves his hand and PETER'S ranting is drowned out by the cries of "Glory to the sovereigns!" "Glory to Russia!" The music booms forth with bravura.*)

IVAN: (*whining and covering his ears*) Make it stop! Make it stop!
(*BORIS GOLITSYN clasps PETER by the shoulders. PETER breaks free. He is still yelling, but his words are drowned out by the din. Exit VASILI GOLITSYN, shaking his head. Curtain. But the music and the cries of "Glory to the sovereigns! Glory to Russia!" can still be heard.*)

ACT 2
SCENE 1

(Tsarina Sofia's chambers. The curtain has not yet risen, but an "old-time" voice can be heard singing.)

OLD-TIME VOICE: The first day in the month of August in the seven thousand one hundred and nine-ty-seventh summer since the creation of the world. The second hour of the sun's rising on this the first day of the first week of August, in the chambers of the great and glorious Princess Sofia Alekseyevna, sitting in privy council . . .

(The "old-time" voice fades, to be replaced with a "contemporary" voice. This voice is expressionless, mechanical, and sounds like an overdubbed translation.)

CONTEMPORARY VOICE: Minutes of the secret meeting of the government committee held on 1 August 1689. Participants: head of state Tsarina S. A. Romanova, head of government V. V. Golitsyn, head of armed forces F. L. Shaklovity, bodyguard A. Tryokhglazov. Topics of discussion: issues relating to domestic policy.

(Meanwhile the curtain rises. There is nothing feminine about the tsarina's bright, airy living chamber, which looks more like a study. SOFIA sits at the crossbar of a T-shaped table. VASILI GOLITSYN and FYODOR SHAKLOVITY sit facing each other on either side of the stem of the T. TRYOKHGLAZOV stands at a certain distance behind GOLITSYN. A scribe sits at a small table to the rear.)

SOFIA: So that's what he said? Who are you to sit in judgement? In front of everybody?

VASILI GOLITSYN: He was screaming and swearing. I won't repeat what. Yes, he's no longer a child. And he hates us with a passion.

SOFIA: The pup! In fact, no, the wolf cub! He has grown up, but we, what with all our other worries, were not paying attention. This is a dangerous malady. As if the state were not in turmoil already. What are we to do? (*To the SCRIBE*) No need to write any of that. Get out! (*The SCRIBE bows and backs out of the room*) What say you, Fyodor Leontyevich? Guarding the state against turmoil is your job.

SHAKLOVITY: (*pointing at TRYOKHGLAZOV*) Let him go out too. What we have to say is not for other people's ears.

SOFIA: No. He must be around Vasili Vasilyevich everywhere and at all times. On my orders.

SHAKLOVITY: (*with a shrug*) As you wish . . . Tell me prince, aren't you alarming the princess for nothing? I have my little men in the Preobrazhensky. They report to me weekly. If anybody is stirring up trouble, it's Petrov's mother, Princess Natalia. According to my spies, the lad is daft, empty-headed. All he wants to do is drink German wine, go sailing, and play at marching with the grooms to the beat of a drum.

VASILI GOLITSYN: I know what spies are like. They always report the things their superiors want to hear. No, the tsar has grown up. And he won't put up with his present position much longer. My cousin Boris has warned me of as much. Princess, I fear your plan for Peter will come to nothing. There is not enough time. And besides, Peter won't go along with it. He's not the type.

SHAKLOVITY: What plan is this?
   (*SOFIA and GOLITSYN exchange glances. The prince nods to the princess.*)

SOFIA: I'm not stupid, Fyodor. I have long known that Ivan's brother would one day grow up and want to become a real tsar. The law is on his side, and a woman ruler is like a mote in the eye. There is only one way out of it. If an heir were born to the elder Tsar Ivan, the child could be declared tsar. Ivan himself could go to a monastery, Peter would be thwarted. And Vasili Vasilyevich and I would raise the little tsar. We would pass on to him a strong and rejuvenated state, we ourselves would . . . But this is no concern of yours.

SHAKLOVITY: It's a good plan, but there's just one snag. Tsar Ivan may be married, but only in appearance. How could the wretch sire children? I doubt his poor queen has even been to bed with him.

SOFIA: I know all that. The wife has had a child with some careless young fellow, but it was a baby girl, worse luck. The second time it will be a son, God willing.

VASILI GOLITSYN: I'm telling you: there's no time for any of this. And Peter won't give up the crown. He's insane.

SHAKLOVITY: You're soft, Vasili Vasilyevich. That's not the way to handle him. Madmen require a firm approach. They calm down if you're firm. Why don't you summon me to the court of your beloved brother, my lady? I'll take a look at him, talk to him. Maybe the devil is not so terrible as he is painted.

SOFIA: Very well then, Fyodor Leontyevich, go. Petrusha is a wolf cub, you are the mother wolf. Take a look at him, sound out his mind. It is the young Tsarina Yevdokiya's name day. You will take her a present from me.

VASILI GOLITSYN: And take my man with you: Anikey Tryokhglazov.

SHAKLOVITY: (*with a smile*) To keep an eye on me? You've grown suspicious. You weren't like this before.

VASILI GOLITSYN: It was you who taught me. (*To TRYOKHGLAZOV*) I'll manage without you for one day; it won't kill me. Observe and remember. I have faith in your eyes and your senses.

SOFIA: Very well, Fyodor, go. Let the warden of the mint enter now. We wish to talk to him about the rouble's rate of exchange with the thaler.

SCENE 2

(*Residence of Tsar Peter in the Preobrazhensky. In front of the lowered curtain, a German OFFICER is drilling a line of his "toy soldiers". They all wear identical blue kaftans with white crosswise harnesses. A piper pipes and a drummer drums, both of them ineptly. TSAR PETER stands to one side, impatiently tapping time with his cane. He wears a cocked hat, a blue kaftan, tall boots, and a sword.*)

OFFICER: *Antreten! Augen-rechts! Gerade-aus! Ein-zwei-drei! Ein-zwei-drei! Kehrt-um!*
  (*The men attempt to make an about-turn, but fall out of line.*)

TSAR PETER: (*taking the drummer's drum*) Give that here! (*Banging the drum*) Like this! Like this!

OFFICER: *Ein-zwei-drei! Ein-zwei-drei! Links! Links!*
  (*The men march in ragged file, a clumsy young lad keeps tripping up.*)

TSAR PETER: (*shoves the drum back at the drummer,*

93

whacks him on the back with his cane) Drum properly,
you son of a bitch!

   (*PETER runs to the file of men, falls in line at their
head, diligently marches, jerking his long legs. He man-
ages to march faster than the rest, who scurry to keep up.*)

OFFICER: *Schneller! Schneller!*

TSAR PETER: He said "shnelluh", you loons! Are you
doing it on purpose, or what? Quick march after me!

   (*The men do their utmost to march in step with the tsar,
and they even start to get the hang of it.*)

TSAR PETER: Look, *kapitan*! This is how it's done!

   (*The young lad stumbles and falls.*)

OFFICER: Nein, Herr Peter, not like ziss. *Muß mann
Geduld haben.* I voss talking. Not everysink at once.

   (*PETER flies into a rage. He rushes over to the lad on
the ground, starts beating him with his cane, growing
more and more furious. He beats him over the head,
all over his body.*)

TSAR PETER: Humiliate me, would you? In front of
the German! You did it on purpose! I'll kill you!

   (*Enter BORIS GOLITSYN. He runs over to the tsar
and grabs him by the shoulders.*)

BORIS GOLITSYN: Beat him, but why kill him? If you

killed every fool in the land, there would be nobody left. Pyotr Alexeyevich, cool off . . . (*He signals to the OFFICER.*)

OFFICER: (*in a loud whisper*) *Gerade-aus! Schneller! Links! Links!*
  (*The toy soldiers retreat into the wings, followed by the piper and the drummer. The young lad brings up the rear, hobbling and groaning.*)

TSAR PETER: Dolts . . . dimwits . . . chuckleheads . . . I hate them! I hate the lumpen Russian! How hard can it be to walk in step? They can't do it! Bickering, chattering, dozing before dinner is all they ever want to do. A flock of sheep! Boris, why did I have to have a people like this? What did I do to deserve it?

BORIS GOLITSYN: Pyotr Alexeyevich, you're a little like my brother Vasili. To him, our people are no good: stupid, benighted, cowardly. And to me and you it's the same. But it's not just his people.

TSAR PETER: (*gradually calming down*) What?

BORIS GOLITSYN: Take this for example. What are you teaching them for?

TSAR PETER: Marching?

BORIS GOLITSYN: Yes, marching. Imagine the whole of Russia marching in step: left-right, left-right. The ground would shake, Europe would cower. The people need law and order. Law and order must be like iron. If a flock of sheep has good sheepdogs, it may be called an army. And with a good shepherd, it may be called a great power. An empire.

TSAR PETER: I love law and order! Everything orderly! Everything like it's supposed to be! Everything in its proper place! Houses all in a neat row, everything inside the houses in regulation order, clothes, work, play all by the book, everything! And no idle thoughts in people's heads, but only the cause! The national cause!

BORIS GOLITSYN: Yes, well, there's no way you can get inside their hearts and minds . . . Why? Because there's nothing of interest in their minds, nor should there be. As for their hearts . . . Vasili suffers on account of the fact that he has made life easier for the people, but they don't love him. That's because Vasili, no matter how clever he might be, doesn't understand one damned thing. Is this what the people really love us for?

TSAR PETER: Then for what?

BORIS GOLITSYN: Did your teachers not teach you what is Russia's joy?

TSAR PETER: "Russia's joy is drink, without drink, Russia would sink". Vladimir Krasnoe Solnyshko said that.

BORIS GOLITSYN: He was a benighted fool. That's why Kiev did not last, but went under. Moscow will not go under, however. Russia's joy is greatness, sire. Our Russian will sit in a wretched hovel eating dry crusts, you can beat him with the knout, take away his children, but give him greatness and he will forgive you all of that. And he will love you for the sake of greatness.

TSAR PETER: (*takes off his cap and waves it in the air*) I'll give Russia greatness! If nothing else, I'll give her greatness!

WOMAN'S VOICE: Petrusha, put your cap back on!

TSAR PETER: (*waving her away*) Oh, Mummy! (*To BORIS*) No peace from these women! Mother is a fool, the wife of a fool, worse even than Sonya.

BORIS GOLITSYN: Well, Sonya's not a fool . . .

TSAR PETER: I hate her! You told me I wouldn't have long to wait.

BORIS GOLITSYN: It won't be long. Like the German said: "Not everysink at once". Soon Russia will be yours. You'll see.

TSAR PETER: But how? Where from? Sonya has got it all: soldiers, guns, treasure. All I've got is this stupid toy army . . . (*Jerks his head in the direction whence can be heard the pipe and drum.*)

WOMAN'S VOICE: Petrusha, your cap!

BORIS GOLITSYN: For the Princess Sofia, the mind and the fist are two separate things. The mind is my cousin, the wonderful dreamer. The fist is Fyodor Shaklovity, the cast-iron noggin. Our task is to wait for the fist to step out of line with the mind and do something reckless. You'll see, this is exactly what's going to happen.

TSAR PETER: All this waiting . . . I can't wait any longer. I refuse to wait . . . I'm seventeen years old already!

WOMAN'S VOICE: Petrusha, you'll get sunstroke!

TSAR PETER: I'm sick of it!
   (*Looks into the wings*)

TSAR PETER: March in step, you swine!
   (*He runs offstage, brandishing his cane. BORIS GOLITSYN runs after him. The curtain parts.*)

SCENE 3

(*Royal Chambers in the Preobrazhensky. Dilapidated wooden chambers. On stage there are two tsarinas. One is middle-aged: NATALYA KIRILLOVNA, Peter's mother; the other a mere girl: his wife, YEVDOKIYA. Both are dressed in festive garb, powdered and made up. They stand next to a table on which gifts are laid out. The sound of the pipe and drum floats through the window.*)

TSARINA YEVDOKIYA: (*takes a handheld mirror from a box*) Oh, look, Mummy, how lovely! The English merchants sent me this.

(*She gazes into the mirror delightedly.*)

TSARINA NATALYA: (*takes the mirror, gazes at herself, adjusts her hair*) A good mirror, a flattering one. It makes you look younger. I'll have this. What do you need to look younger for, you're young already . . .

TSARINA YEVDOKIYA: Mummy! Natalya Kirillovna! You've already taken the Venetian lace, the mother-of-pearl tiara, the ermine jacket. Let me have the mirror at least!

(*She tries to take the mirror back.*)

TSARINA NATALYA: I'm not taking it forever. Only for a while. When I die, I'll leave everything to you.

TSARINA YEVDOKIYA: (*with a sigh*) Take it then. Maybe I'd been dreaming of having a mirror . . .

TSARINA NATALYA: There she goes again, talking about dreams! How much more?

TSARINA YEVDOKIYA: Isn't this a dream? I was just a young girl, called Parasha Lopukhina, I lived with my father and mother. All of a sudden, they took me from my house to the royal chambers, nipped me, tweaked me, dressed me, undressed me, like a doll. They said: You will be the tsarina of all Russia. They would marry me off to somebody or other. The first time I saw him was in church. Just a wee lad, three years younger than me, with down on his upper lip. Spraying slobber, twitching, reeking of tobacco water. They say: You are no longer Praskovya Illarionovna, a nobleman's daughter. You are now Yevdokiya Fyodorovna, a tsarina. And who is this "Yevdokiya Fyodorovna, a tsarina"? Maybe it's not me at all. Maybe I'm dreaming the whole thing . . .

TSARINA NATALYA: Foolish girl! Should I pinch her to wake her up?
    (*She pinches her.*)

TSARINA YEVDOKIYA: Ow!

TSARINA NATALYA: Woken up at last? Or shall I do it again?

TSARINA YEVDOKIYA: (*rubbing the spot where she was pinched*) I'm awake . . . Well, if I'm not asleep and I'm really the tsarina, give me back my presents!
    (*She snatches the mirror from the table*)

TSARINA YEVDOIYA: I'm the tsarina of the living tsar, but who are you? A widow? Get thee to a nunnery! Pray to the icons! What do you need a mirror for? Give me back that tiara, too! And the sheepskin jerkin!
    (*The two women play tug-o'-war with the gifts.*)

SOLEMN VOICE OFF-STAGE: The head of the Streltsy Department, Fyodor Shaklovity, will now attend Her Royal Majesty Tsarina Yevdokiya.

TSARINA NATALYA: (*cowers in fear*) The cutthroat Fedka Shaklovity! What is he doing here? Seven years ago, he murdered my brothers Afony and Vanya! The Streltsy burned them alive! And now he wants me dead too! Fear him! Don't argue with him!
    (*Both women sit down, assuming a dignified posture. Enter Shaklovity with a bow. He looks around him grimly.*)

SHAKLOVITY: I trust your royal highnesses are in

good health? The Empress Sofia Alekseyevna wishes you many summers and sends you a gift on your name day.

(Clicks his fingers. TRYOKHGLAZOV appears and hands him an icon.)

SHAKLOVITY: The icon of Saint Yevdokiya, Holy Martyr, beheaded by the Latin pagans.

(He gives the icon to YEVDOKIYA, who shrinks back in her chair and quickly puts it to one side. SHAKLOVITY clicks his fingers once more. TRYOKHGLAZOV hands him a bundle tied with ribbon.)

SHAKLOVITY: *(to TSARINA NATALYA)* There is also a gift for you, Natalya Kirillovna. The empress wishes you to have vestments in keeping with your station.

(He takes a nun's cassock from the bundle.)

SHAKLOVITY: Sofia Alekseyevna knows that you will be retiring to a nunnery. A blessed, godly decision. It was also time.

(Tsarina Natalya jumps up and backs away, toward the window.)

TSARINA NATALYA: Petrusha! Petrusha!

(The pipe and drum have fallen silent. SHAKLOVITY calmly turns to face the wings, whence PETER comes running.)

PETER: What is it, Mummy?

(*He sees SHAKLOVITY and freezes.*)

PETER: You! What are you doing here?

TSARINA NATALYA: Petya, they're taking me to a nunnery! Petya!

SHAKLOVITY: (*with a casual bow*) Hullo there, Peter Alekseyevich. What are you dressed up as a German for? That's no good. My streltsy are unhappy. They say the young tsar doesn't love us Russian warriors, he much prefers German stuff. You know what the streltsy are like. I'm their leader, but even I am afraid of them. When they're enraged, there's no holding them back. Remember when they broke into the palace and tore your uncles to bits? God forbid it happen again. Be so kind as to listen to the advice of a faithful servant, your majesty. Please put on Russian clothes and come with me to Moscow. We'll travel with your troops, you'll say a few kind words to the streltsy, you'll give them new wine. You'll see, they'll cool off . . .

(*Listening to SHAKLOVITY, PETER begins to twitch, more and more noticeably, more and more violently.*)

PETER: (*in a falsetto voice, choking with fury*) Are . . . you . . . telling me what to do? Are you threatening me with the streltsy? You dog! You didn't finish me off when I was little, and now you're going to try? I'm not the same as I was then . . . No, not that! I'm not a cat!

SHAKLOVITY: No, not a cat? Of course you're not a cat. If I'm a dog, then you're a kitten.

PETER: (*turning around*) Preobrazhensky guards! To me! (*Two stalwart young fellows, the PREOBRAZHENSKY GUARDS run in, wearing tunics like PETER'S, with white crosswise bandoliers.*)

PETER: Seize him! To the dungeon with him!

SHAKLOVITY: Are you out of your mind, sire? (*He falls back.*)

PETER: (*panting*) Wh . . . where? Seize him! (*The PREOBRAZHENSKY GUARDS grab SHAKLOVITY by the armpits.*)

SHAKLOVITY: How the cockerel squawks! There are twenty thousand streltsy in Moscow. They'll tear this palace down, stone by stone. They'll smash this chicken coop of yours with all the chickens in it!

PETER: Me? A cockerel? You're calling me a cockerel? Cut him down, lads! Let me . . . let me at him! (*He is about to draw his sword, but has a seizure. He staggers backward, his throat rattles, he topples over, his heels beat against the floor. YEVDOKIYA screams.*)

TSARINA NATALYA: Not again! Petenka!

(She rushes to her son, but cannot stop him thrashing around.)

(TRYOKHGLAZOV, who has been standing still all the while, now approaches the PREOBRAZHENSKY GUARDS.)

TRYOKHGLAZOV: Don't just stand there, you fools! Hold the tsar down before he injures himself!

(The GUARDS rush over to PETER. TRYOKHGLAZOV grabs SHAKLOVITY by the arm and drags him away. They vanish amid PETER'S inarticulate yells, TSARINA YEVDOKIYA'S screeches, and TSARINA NATALYA'S wails.)

SCENE 4

(The Princess Sofia's chambers. A stormy night. From time to time, thunder rolls and lightning flashes. The wind gusts and the rain lashes.)

(The curtain rises to reveal SOFIA, VASILI GOLITSYN and SHAKLOVITY sitting in exactly the same places as in Act Two, Scene Two, except that it is now night and candles have been lit: the princess is at the head of the table, the ministers opposite each other, and the bodyguard at a discreet distance behind the prince.)

VASILI GOLITSYN: And now, Fyodor Leontyevich, let me tell you exactly the same thing you told me just now. Aren't you being rather over the top?

SHAKLOVITY: Over the top? You should have seen his face! He's a ravening wild beast! If it hadn't been for your man, prince, he would have cut me down with his sword. A decision has to be made. And fast. Any delay, and it'll be too late. It's going to end up bloody. Very bloody. And the longer we draw it out, the bloodier it will be . . . Let me put it another way: it's all a question of whose blood gets spilled, his or ours.

VASILI GOLITSYN: Get a grip on yourself, Fyodor! Of whose blood do you speak? The tsar's! And what is he? A boy. What can he do? What power does he have? A toy army of two hundred men. And do not forget: We are not villains, we are not conspirators. We are the law. We are the state.

SHAKLOVITY: It's all very well you giving sermons. It's not your head he's going to separate from your shoulders, Prince Golitsyn. I'm the one who'll be thrown in the torture chamber, put on the rack, and then given to the axe. Well, I'm not a sheep to submit so meekly! Princess, today I have gathered together my trusty captains. At the same time, everyone is ready, there is nothing to fear. Merely give the order.

   (*SOFIA sits motionless. She looks first at SHAKLOVITY, then at VASILI GOLITSYN.*)

SHAKLOVITY: Vasili Vasilyevich, you talk of a beautiful Russia, you promise her prosperity. If Peter reigns, none of this will happen. He's a halfwit! If he is in power, gibbets will fill Red Square, the streltsy will hang from the walls of the Kremlin! It will be like in the time of Ivan the Terrible again!

VASILI GOLITSYN: You cannot build prosperity on the ruin of the soul. Godunov tried it, after murdering the young Prince Dmitri. You know very well how it turned out. He destroyed his own soul, wasted away, perished.

SHAKLOVITY: Empress, what do you have to say? Show firmness. That Peter won't spare you. Locked up in a dungeon to the end of your days, wasting away, never to be released. As far as I'm concerned, better the axe. Don't you understand? It's either you or him; there's no third option. You don't give me any specific undertaking. You merely say, "Do whatever you think necessary, Fyodor". I'll handle everything personally. Everything is prepared. Shall I spell it out? But at least why don't you say something!

SOFIA: (*suddenly turning to TRYOKHGLAZOV*) What about you? What do you think?

TRYOKHGLAZOV: For three years, our association camped on the bank of the Amur River. It was good there. Secluded. Lots of birds, fish, grassy meadows. Only one problems: multitudes of snakes. They bit all the horses. And horses are expensive in Siberia.

SHAKLOVITY: He has the time to tell rambling stories.

SOFIA: One moment, Fyodor Leontyevich. Well? Go on.

TRYOKHGLAZOV: We smote and we smote the

snakes, but still there were more. And so, I walk down the path. I see a little snake. It's still a baby, it can't move fast. It opens its jaws, and the fangs are still tiny. It's like an infant, but it will grow. God forbid!

SOFIA: What then?

TRYOKHGLAZOV: I crushed it, of course. Should I let them live, let their fangs grow, let them fill with venom?

VASILI GOLITSYN: A human being, and even less so a tsar, is not a serpent.

TRYOKHGLAZOV: A human being, and even more so a tsar, is far more dangerous than a serpent.

SHAKLOVITY: Listen to him, Vasili Vasilyevich. He's gold. Finally, you have a practical man around you, rather than all those talkers. You want to build a marvellous city wearing immaculate white clothes. It's not going to happen. Building means dust and mud. The washing and cleaning comes afterwards. Don't fret, prince, you won't dirty your hands. Everything will work out just fine without you. But give me your bodyguard. He'll come in handy.

(*Stands up and approaches TRYOKHGLAZOV*)

SHAKLOVITY: Anikey, my young streltsy are warlike,

but not bright, whereas you are a clever, experienced man. Will you be able to kill the serpent in such a way as not to give yourself away?

TRYOKHGLAZOV: If the prince orders it, I will kill him.

SHAKLOVITY: Then it will be a clean job!
  (*Turns to the princess.*)

SHAKLOVITY: Listen, princess: this is how it will be done. Anikey will go there and kill the serpent. I will raise the alarm to the streltsy. I will announce that malefactors in the Preobrazhensky have killed Tsar Peter. Come, let us eliminate the Naryshkins and the toy army. And if Anikey fails, we'll finish the lad off. He'll have no escape. The streltsy will stand down later. The plan is sound, princess, it cannot fail. Merely nod your head!

TRYOKHGLAZOV: I do not serve the princess. I serve the prince.
  (*They look at VASILI GOLITSYN, who remains silent.*)

SOFIA: Both of you leave the room. Leave me alone with Prince Vasili.
  (*SHAKLOVITY, looking behind him at every step, leaves the room. TRYOKHGLAZOV goes out without looking back.*)

SOFIA: Vasya, remember how you used to talk to me seven

years ago? It was just the same. Whether I should rise up against the Naryshkins or not. Whether I should remain a little girl-princess or fight for power . . . I would cry, I was afraid: who was I to wield power? Do you remember?

VASILI GOLITSYN: You shouldn't think back on it. You were just a little girl. Your lips would tremble. My heart was torn with pity. But it was impossible to back down. The villainous Naryshkins would have stolen the land, looted it.

SOFIA: (*going over to him*) I used to say to you that I did not know how to rule. That I did not know what it was to rule. You would say, "Power is very difficult, but also very simple. You need to stop thinking about yourself, that's all there is to it. Your body is the whole country. If it has a fever then you have a fever. If it aches then you ache. Your soul is the people. If the people finds salvation then your soul finds salvation. If the people finds perdition then your soul finds perdition". That's what you said to me back then. And now you are afraid your own soul will find perdition. Where is your soul, Vasya? What is it like? Is it small? Does it reside here?
(*She points at his chest*)

SOFIA: Or is it big, residing here?
(*She makes a sweeping gesture with her hand. A clap of thunder. VASILI GOLITSYN remains silent, his head bowed.*)

SOFIA: (*plaintively*) What am I to do? Who am I? Am I the ruler on whose shoulders rests the power of thousands of versts, from the Swedish Sea to the Chinese Ocean? Or am I a woman to whom your little soul is dearer than anything else in the world? Tell me, Vasya. I will do whatever is best for you.

(*VASILI remains silent.*)

SOFIA: Because they will separate us. We'll never see each other again. You often say: "History, history. How will you and I go down in history? The ruler and her lover who kept neither their country nor each other?" Speak, Vasya. Don't be silent.

(*VASILI remains silent.*)

SOFIA: There is one other thing I learned about power, something you didn't finish telling me about before it arrived by itself. A ruler is one who is able to bring about the terrible. And the larger soul, the soul of power, is more important to him than his own. But if your own soul is dearer, better you leave. I will not leave, however. Both for the sake of the state and for your sake. Do not say anything to your Tryokhglazov. We can do without him. God willing, the streltsy will manage. Do not torture yourself, Vasya. Save your own soul. I know you will gnaw away at yourself afterward. There's no need. I will take care of everything. Come what may in the next world. God will either forgive me or He won't. His will be done.

VASILI GOLITSYN: (*lifting his head*) No! If we are together, then we are together!

　(*A gust of wind blows open the window. The sound of the storm crashes through. The candles are snuffed out. Darkness falls over the stage.*)

SCENE 5

(*The Preobrazhensky. By the pond. Evening. BORIS GOLITSYN and PETER stand in a boat by the jetty. BORIS GOLITSYN holds a ship's wheel, PETER looks at a plan.*)

PETER: How is it inserted?

BORIS GOLITSYN: My lord, let us go to bed. It's late.

PETER: Go to bed? What, now? Look at this beauty that master craftsman Kraus has made me! A real ship's wheel! Worthy of a frigate! Give it here!
(*He takes the wheel and tries to mount it.*)

BORIS GOLITSYN: This boat is old, unseaworthy. And you can't sail here on the pond. Let's go to Lake Pleshcheyevo. We'll test it there. And after that we'll build real frigates. And not only frigates. We'll build three-decked ships. Look out Turkey! Get ready, Europe! The Russian flag is on its way!

PETER: We'll sink them with broadsides!

BORIS GOLITSYN: If they don't get out of our way, we'll blow them out of the water!

PETER: And I'll build a new capital by the sea, on an empty shore! I hate Moscow and its stupid wooden buildings and crooked streets. I'll build my city in precisely the right place. Everything will be at right angles, by regulation! That's where I'll live!

BORIS GOLITSYN: As you command, sire, so it will be done. The land will be like a seagoing vessel: it will sail where the captain orders.

(PETER finishes mounting the ship's wheel.)

PETER: Captain's orders! Hoist the flag! Full speed ahead! Fire the cannons!

(A gunshot. PETER falls out of the boat. He takes a few steps forward, falls once more. TRYOKHGLAZOV appears from offstage, hiding a gun in his girdle.)

BORIS GOLITSYN: Argh! Sire! Petrusha!

(He rushes to PETER. Then he turns to the assassin and hurls himself at him.)

BORIS GOLITSYN: How dare you raise your hand against him! Villain!

(TRYOKHGLAZOV whirls his whip, lassoes GOLITSYN'S neck, jerks him to the ground. He hits him over the head.)

TRYOKHGLAZOV: Lie still, boyar. The order is not to kill you.

(He walks toward PETER. He takes a second pistol from his belt. The tsar tries to lift himself up, clenches his fist. TRYOKHGLAZOV shoots him in the head.)

TRYOKHGLAZOV: There. The serpent will bite no more.

(Exit, calmly, without haste. Groaning, BORIS GOLITSYN picks himself up. He staggers over to the slain man. He kneels down beside him.)

BORIS GOLITSYN: My lord! Slain, slain . . . Now there will be nothing. Nothing to dream of. No fleet. No victories. No window on Europe. No regulation capital on the seashore. No empire . . . No greatness for Russia . . .

(Sobs bitterly. The curtain falls behind him. Spotlight on the dead PETER and the grieving boyar. Strains of a funeral march. The spotlight fades. Pause. There must be a full sense of the performance being over.)

VOICE OF SOFIA: Come what may in the next world. God will either forgive me or He won't. His will be done.

VOICE OF VASILI GOLITSYN: No! If we are together, then we are together!

(The wind roars. The sound of a window flying open with a crash.)

SCENE 6

(Princess SOFIA'S chambers. The curtain rises. Frozen time flows once more. The stage is in darkness. The wind howls. The sound of the window being closed. The din of the storm abates. A light flares. The candles are lit one by one. It is VASILI GOLITSYN who has closed the window. SOFIA has lit the candles. The previously interrupted scene continues.)

SOFIA: So you agree?

VASILI GOLITSYN: Agree to what? To stand to one side and wash my hands of it? To let you take the sin wholly upon yourself? And who will I be after that? How will I live? No!

SOFIA: "Who will *I* be"? "How will *I* live"? You're thinking about yourself? Not about the country? Not about the people? Not about me?

VASILI GOLITSYN: About you, about me and you . . . It is not what I taught you. I was wrong. The soul is

117

neither big nor small. It is the soul. Be not deceived. There is nothing in the world for whose sake you should destroy your soul. Have you forgotten the Gospel? "For what is a man profited, if he shall gain the whole world, and lose his own soul? Or what shall a man give in exchange for his soul?" What will happen will happen. And if we are not destined to be together in this world, nobody will part us in the next.

SOFIA: (*softly*) Let it be the best for you . . .
    (*They embrace.*)

SCENE 7

(At the Preobrazehnsky again. By the pond. Everything is exactly as it was at the beginning of Act Two, Scene Five. BORIS GOLITSYN and PETER stand in a boat by the jetty. BORIS GOLITSYN holds a ship's wheel, PETER looks at a plan.)

PETER: How is it inserted?

BORIS GOLITSYN: My lord, let us go to bed. It's late.

PETER: Go to bed? What, now? Look at this beauty that master craftsman Kraus has made me! A real ship's wheel! Worthy of a frigate! Give it here!
(He takes the wheel and tries to mount it.)

BORIS GOLITSYN: This boat is old, unseaworthy. And you can't sail here on the pond. Let's go to Lake Pleshcheyevo. We'll test it there. And after that we'll build real frigates. And not only frigates. We'll build three-decked ships. Look out Turkey! Get ready, Europe! The Russian flag is on its way!

PETER: We'll sink them with broadsides!

BORIS GOLITSYN: If they don't get out of our way, we'll blow them out of the water!

PETER: And I'll build a new capital by the sea, on an empty shore! I hate Moscow and its stupid wooden buildings and crooked streets. I'll build my city in precisely the right place. Everything will be at right angles, by regulation! That's where I'll live!

BORIS GOLITSYN: As you command, sire, so it will be done. The land will be like a seagoing vessel: it will sail where the captain orders.
    (*PETER finishes mounting the ship's wheel.*)

PETER: Captain's orders! Hoist the flag! Full speed ahead! Fire the cannons!
    (*Enter TRYOKHGLAZOV from the wings.*)

TRYOKHGLAZOV: Sire! Trouble! The streltsy are on their way from Moscow. Shaklovity has sent them to kill you! Save yourself!

PETER: Oh! What? Boris . . . Where? To the Trinity! Escape! Boris, the horse!
    (*He is delirious. BORIS grabs him, holds him back.*)

BORIS GOLITSYN: One moment, my man . . . Who

are you? I've seen you before! You're one of Vasili's men!

TRYOKHGLAZOV: I'm my own man.

BORIS GOLITSYN: Are the streltsy far away?

TRYOKHGLAZOV: The alarm has been raised.

BORIS GOLITSYN: That means they're still far away.
They're not Germans to be able to harness their horses
quickly.
   (*Slaps his thigh.*)

BORIS GOLITSYN: What luck! Oh, how glorious!

PETER: What do you mean, luck? What's got into you?
They want to kill me!

BORIS GOLITSYN: They want to, but they won't.
There is time, sire. We'll muster and go to the Trinity,
under the protection of fortress walls. From there we
will proclaim to the whole country that Sofia wanted
to get rid of Tsar Peter and that you barely escaped. The
princess is finished. She rose against the lawful ruler. We
win. Russia is yours, sire!

PETER: Is it?

BORIS GOLITSYN: No doubt about it now. It will

be all yours. Everything we talked about: the fleet, the victories, the new capital on a deserted shore. You will be Peter the Great! Russia will be great!

PETER: I will be great? Peter the Great?

BORIS GOLITSYN: (*to TRYOKHGLAZOV*) Why are you not with Vasili instead of here with me?

TRYOKHGLAZOV: I am like water. Water does not flow uphill. Better with you in whatever way than with him in any way at all.

PETER: I will be great! Russia will be great! Hoorah!
   (*PETER straightens his shoulders. He raises his arm, holding the rolled-up chart. His other hand clutches the ship's wheel. The boat suddenly starts to rise into the air. PETER freezes and turns into Tsereteli's monument. A victory march, the rumble of cannon volleys. Curtain.*)

About the Author

Boris Akunin (pen-name of Grigory Chkhartishvili, b. 1956) is best known as a writer of genre (mainly detective) fiction, he is also the author of literary fiction, books on history, plays and essays. His recent popular history project, "History of the Russian State", combines volumes of non-fiction and fiction. Akunin's books have sold more than 30 million copies in Russia alone and have been translated into almost 50 languages. A number of his works have been adapted in Russia for cinema and television.

About the Translator

Ileana Alexandra Orlich is President's Professor of Comparative Literature and Romanian Studies at Arizona State University. Her publications examine the societies and cultures of Central and Eastern Europe. She is also a translator of fiction and drama. Her translations of plays have been staged in New York and Bucharest.